How to ComplaiN

Christopher Ward is Assistant Editor of the *Sunday Mirror* and also writes a humorous magazine column which is syndicated world-wide. This is his first book.

Frank Dickens is one of Britain's most popular cartoonists, best known for his 'Bristow' strip cartoon which appears in newspapers and magazines all over the world.

Christopher War d

How to Complain

revised edition

illustrated by Frank Dickens

Pan Books London and Sydney

Originally published in Great Britain 1974 by
Martin Secker & Warburg Ltd
and 1976 by Pan Books Ltd, Cavaye Place, London SW10 9PG
Revised edition first published 1979 by
Martin Secker & Warburg Ltd
This edition published 1980 by Pan Books Ltd
text © Christopher Ward 1974, 1976, 1979
illustrations © Frank Dickens 1974
ISBN 0 330 25947 4
Printed and bound in Great Britain by
Richard Clay (The Chaucer Press) Ltd, Bungay, Suffolk

The Government is not a wet-nurse to every customer.
Some people will have to take action to look after themselves.

– *Lord Lever*

Where the broom does not reach, the dust will not vanish of itself.

– *Mao Tse-Tung*

CONTENTS

INTRODUCTION

This book is for people who have been trying unsuccessfully to get a plumber round to look at their radiators for the past two years. It's for people whose new car has broken down nineteen times and whose laundry feeds their clothes through a shirt-shredding and button-crushing machine. It's for people who can't get through to Train Enquiries and who can't catch a waiter's eye.

That's about everyone, isn't it?

It tells you, simply, how to get things done. How to get past the officious clerk on the housing department counter or the managing director's over-protective secretary. How to prosecute the M1 maniac who overtook you on the inside at 90 mph. How to twist a computer's arm (yes, *arm*) so that it treats you as a human being and not just another number. It tells you who to complain to when the gas board cuts off your supply two weeks after you paid the bill, and how to give your stroppy bank manager a sleepless night or two.

There are conventional ways of dealing with all these problems, of course, only few of us live that long. This book tells you all the short cuts.

You've tried asking nicely, and that didn't work, so from now on, you must consider yourself at war. The enemy are all those people out there who take your money and then don't come up with their part of the deal. They are the inefficient, the slothful, the rude, the men and women of 1001 excuses and 1002 broken promises.

This is a consumer guerrilla warfare manual. Use it to spread fear and confusion among the ranks of the enemy.

You don't have to be Someone to win. You don't need a public-school accent. You don't even need a new suit. All you need is determination.

This book is also for the enemy. While there's still time for them to come out with their hands up.

The address and telephone number of every organization mentioned in this book is listed at the back on page 260.

ANATOMY OF A COMPLAINT

A complaint can vary in scale and intensity from a bang on the ceiling with a broom-handle to a four-month High Court hearing. Before you start complaining, you must therefore

1 ASK yourself what you are complaining about and identify the enemy.
2 FIND OUT your legal rights.
3 DECIDE whether the cause is worth a full-scale war or just a local skirmish.
4 DRAW UP a battle plan to defeat the enemy.

EXAMPLE: A transistor radio is playing loudly next to you on the beach.
ACTION: Ask the irritant to turn it off or lower the volume.
RESULT: (a) Victory.
(b) Volume is only slightly lowered, thus necessitating further complaint.
(c) Refusal.

In the event of a refusal (*c*) there are several alternatives open to you:

SOLUTION ONE: Throw the transistor radio into the sea.
SOLUTION TWO: Call the police and make an official complaint.
SOLUTION THREE: Move to another beach.

If you're faint-hearted enough to take Solution Three, you're probably the sort of person who felt obliged to buy this book because a sales assistant caught you thumbing through it. You should have saved your money.

WARD'S LAW: Nothing in the world is difficult for one who sets his mind to it.

ADVERTISEMENTS

Hard though it is to believe, there is a rule that all advertisements must be 'legal, decent, honest and truthful'.

It so happens that Guinness *is* good for you, but if the firm couldn't prove it, there would have to be one hell of a lot of pasting-over of hoardings, not to mention a desperate hunt for a new slogan.

Not all advertisements are as straightforward as the Guinness campaign and many, as you have no doubt discovered to your disadvantage, make extravagant claims that can't be supported and promises that aren't kept. Unfortunately, by the time you find out it's a con – you've been conned.

TOO LATE you discover that the TV rental firm who promised you a 24-hour service in their advertisement take ten days to send an engineer when your set breaks down.

TOO LATE you learn the truth about the miracle acne cure that left you as spotty as it found you.

TOO LATE you find that the car you bought because of its advertised 40-miles-per-gallon petrol consumption just about manages twenty – and that downhill with the wind behind.

If you feel you have been deliberately misled by an advertisement you should write to the firm concerned demanding that they supply you with the goods or service that they promised you – or refund your money. You should add that you have 'taken advice' and that 'there seems to have been an infringement of the Code of Advertising Practice'. They probably won't know what the hell you're talking about, but at least you sound as if you mean business.

Tell them that if you don't receive satisfaction you will refer the matter to the Advertising Standards Authority, but you feel sure that they will wish to avoid involving themselves in the trouble and expense that this would cause them. (If you wish to save others from the same fate as yourself it may be as well to do this anyway, but don't tell the enemy that, or you'll lose your strong bargaining position.)

What is the Advertising Standards Authority? The ASA is the ad industry's own watchdog organization, responsible for making sure all advertisements in newspapers, on posters and on the cinema screen are 'legal, decent, honest and truthful'. It has a Code of Advertising Practice which has to be observed on a scout's honour sort of basis and may demand that an offending advertisement is changed or dropped altogether by the advertisers.

It can't get you your money back, but if there *has* been an infringement of the code it may privately suggest to the advertisers that they do the gentlemanly thing and hand over the cash. Most firms fall into line when they are read the riot act by the ASA.

Write to the Secretary of the ASA giving details of your complaint and enclosing, if possible, a copy of the offending advertisement stating when and where it appeared.

Blatant infringements of the code are acted on immediately by the Secretary. But if he feels the firm concerned has a case, then a council of twelve – eight of whom have nothing to do with the advertising world – consider whether there are grounds for action. Every month the council publishes a report which details the complaints considered and delivers a public kick in the pants – but not much more – to offenders.

The ASA is particularly helpful when mail-order firms fail to come up with the goods (see 'Mail Order') and it also keeps an eye open for well-practised con-tricks in leaflets and price lists.

As a public-spirited, interfering busybody citizen, you are perfectly entitled to draw the ASA's attention to any advertisement even if you haven't had any dealings with the firm.

The ASA doesn't however have any control over TV or radio commercials, so please do *not* send it a pair of your husband's underpants demanding to know why they don't look as white as the underpants washed in Wundersuds on the telly.

Complaints about TV and commercial radio ads should be sent to the Head of Advertising Control at the Independent Broadcasting Authority, who apply much more stringent standards.

What about classified ads? Deals between private individuals are not protected by the law, so beware of the small-ad seller who offers you a parrot with a vocabulary of two thousand words.

WARD'S LAW: Complain now while offence lasts.

AGGRO

(or: how to make a nuisance of yourself)

Guerrillas succeed in getting what they want in the end because they make sure the enemy doesn't get a night's sleep until they do. When all reasonable approaches have failed, you too must make your enemy's life a misery.

Here is where you can hit them the hardest:

EMBARRASS THE ENEMY. If you feel your local council aren't taking enough interest in your garbage problems, dump a dustbin-load on the steps of the town hall ten minutes before a council meeting. You may be prosecuted for depositing litter, but your case – not to mention the town hall – will quickly get a good airing. (Mushroom grower Paul Nixon dumped two tons of horse manure in the middle of Brighton railway station to protest about a parcel British Rail had lost and didn't seem in any hurry to find. In no time at all the entire station staff were on the scent of Mr Nixon's lost parcel.)

WARN would-be customers of the kind of treatment they can expect from the enemy by parading outside their premises with your grievances clearly stated on a banner. As soon as the enemy see you are costing them money they will be only too eager to clear up the 'unfortunate misunderstanding'.

RING UP the chairman or managing director at home. The switchboard girl will give you his name, and if he's not in the telephone book, you can probably trick his secretary

into revealing his home address. Be charming. Tell her you're from Interflora and you have a bouquet for his wife but have mislaid the address.

If one telephone call doesn't succeed, ring him a few more times at inconvenient moments – just as he gets home from work, late at night, or Sunday lunchtime. Write to him at home too. He'll soon tell someone on his staff to get you off his back.

INUNDATE the enemy with letters and telephone calls. Send carbon copies to their head office and to organizations they belong to, so that they are involved in expensive and time-consuming correspondence. Send them telegrams. Arrive at the enemy's headquarters uninvited and create a scene in front of other customers.

DISRUPT the decorum of the company's annual general meeting by asking the chairman when his repair department are going to give you back your telly that they've had for two years.

Any shareholder is entitled to speak at the AGM. How do you become a shareholder? It's as easy as buying a Premium Bond. Well, almost. Ask your bank to buy for you one Ordinary share. This will cost anything from 5p to £10 or more, depending on the Stock Market price. If you don't have a bank account, look up the name of a stockbroker in the Yellow Pages, and ask him to buy a share for you. There is a 'transaction charge' of about £6.

You will get your chance to speak when the chairman announces question time. It might help you to jot down on a piece of paper what you intend to say, so that you don't waffle on. Don't let anyone shut you up, either; as a shareholder it's your right to speak. Mums are always getting up at the Marks and Spencer annual meeting to complain about jammed zip fasteners and rotting shoes. Marks' board of directors, a most democratic body of men, always gives them a fair hearing.

BULLY the enemy into submission. When Professor David Klein, a mild-mannered Michigan academic, arrived at a hotel in Montreal he was told that his reservation could not be honoured, due to a mix-up.

'I will give you three minutes to find me a room,' Professor Klein told the manager, 'then I am going to undress in the lobby, put on my pyjamas and go to sleep on one of the sofas.'

He got his room.

WARD'S LAW: Be ruthless to your enemies.

AIRLINES

An air ticket costs tens, maybe hundreds, of pounds. The flight lasts no longer than a few hours. And at the end of it, you have nothing to show for your money. All you are left with is a used ticket stub and a happy – or an unhappy – memory of the flight.

It is therefore not unreasonable to expect the airlines to meet the few demands we passengers make on them. These are:

1. When we have made a reservation, to keep that seat for us and not to sell it to anyone else.
2. To get us to our destinations safely, comfortably, and more or less on time.
3. To reunite us with our baggage at the other end.

Unhappily airlines, run as they are by fallible humans and computers, sometimes fall down on one or more of these obligations.

From time to time a traveller will find himself stranded in Johannesburg at the very moment his family are waiting for him to arrive at Heathrow, while – for some reason that no one knows – his baggage is winging its way to Tampa, Florida, never to be seen again.

In a situation like this, it may be little consolation to you to know that the airline is very sorry indeed. But it really *is* sorry, and most airlines will go to extraordinary lengths to make amends.

Why? Firstly, because the airline business is highly competitive. Airlines spend millions of pounds every year telling everyone how much more wonderful they are than all their competitors, and every late plane, every lost bag, is a thousand pounds' worth of goodwill and business lost to a rival.

Secondly, because airlines' mistakes cost them more dearly than those of almost any other commercial organization.

It costs £1,000 to lay on lunch at an airport for all the passengers of a delayed Jumbo jet – £5,000 if they have to stay overnight in a hotel. More than £30,000,000 a year is paid out in compensation for lost luggage alone.

I won't go on in case I make you cry. I merely mention it because with sums like these at stake, you can rest assured that someone up there really does care.

Now for the passengers' sob stories . . .

LOST LUGGAGE

Every year the airlines between them manage to mislay several million suitcases, dress bags, hat-boxes, skis, guitars, etc. Most of these are recovered within twenty-four hours but nevertheless an awful lot continue to travel around the world without their owners.

By international agreement, the airlines accept only a limited liability on the luggage they lose. On international flights, compensation is paid according to the weight, not the value – £10.78 per kilo.

This may be adequate compensation for a party of nuns on a package-tour pilgrimage to Lourdes, but it is hardly an adequate pay-out for a suitcase full of Elizabeth Taylor's mink coats.

Airlines will sometimes pay over the odds, but don't bank on it. Best to take out a separate insurance policy.

The chances are, however, that your bags aren't lost, but merely going on a world tour without you. As a result you have to suffer the aggravation of a holiday or a business trip without any of your clothes.

Obviously the inconvenience of being separated from your possessions even for a few hours is an intolerable – and often expensive – one.

You could be stranded in Moscow in the middle of winter with only the cotton frock you were wearing when you left Nassau.

You might be expected at a state banquet at the embassy in Paris in two hours' time – with nothing to wear except the polo-neck sweater and corduroy trousers you travelled in.

In situations like this an airline should cough up something to see you through the crisis. Your bag will probably turn up within 24 hours, so they will probably offer you at least ten quid to buy yourself some wash things and a change of underwear to see you through until tomorrow.

But if you are involved in additional expense – if you have to hire a dinner-jacket, for instance – then you are entitled to ask for more. After all, why should you have to spend the first day of ten days' holiday without a bathing costume to swim in?

Some airlines, mindful of their responsibilities, will make £40 cash payments on the spot for mislaid bags.

Honesty note: It is as well, when making claims against airlines, not to exaggerate the value of the contents of your bag. By the law of averages your bag is bound to arrive at its proper destination one day – and when it is opened it will be discovered that you are dressed by Marks and Spencer of Chipping Norton, and not by Pierre Cardin of Paris.

In fact there's every chance you will be reunited with your baggage, thanks to a computer dating service for lost bags. It's called the Central Baggage Tracing Unit and it's run by Eastern Airlines in Miami, Florida.

If your bags are still missing after 72 hours then the airline you travelled with will send a description of your luggage to Miami where details will be fed into a computer. Meanwhile, if anyone has noticed some 'separated' bags lying around unclaimed for a day or two, a description will be passed on to Miami. With luck, the two sets of details will whirl around in the computer and be matched up. Your luggage will then be returned to you wherever you are.

DOUBLE BOOKING (otherwise known as 'bumping' or 'denied boarding')

Thousands of passengers every year take the precaution of booking their airline ticket well in advance to be sure of a seat. Then they ring up twenty-four hours before the flight to confirm their booking, as all prudent passengers should.

But when they get to the airport, in good time for their flight, they learn that there has been double booking and there is no seat for them on that flight.

Sometimes the airline is able to book a 'bumped' passenger on the next flight an hour later, without causing too much inconvenience. But often there isn't another flight until the next day.

Appointments are missed. Hotel beds that haven't been slept in have to be paid for. Auntie Alice and Uncle Jock drive forty miles to the airport to meet a passenger who isn't on the plane. And you end up spending the night in Hounslow instead of Honolulu.

Bumping can be an innocent mistake. It can be a computer error. But most likely it is caused by an airline deliberately selling more tickets than it has seats on that flight.

It's quite usual, for instance, for an airline to accept seven hundred bookings for one Jumbo flight, knowing – hoping, anyway – that by the day of the flight half the passengers won't turn up, leaving them with one full, profitable plane-load.

It's a kind of Russian roulette – with you as the loser.

Now for the good news: most of the big airlines have agreed to pay a 'no-argument compensation' if you are bumped from a flight leaving the UK. The airline should still try to find you a seat on another flight to your destination, but if you are delayed for more than four hours on international flights, you get the money anyway.

The agreed rate for compensating you for denied boarding is one half of the cost of a one-way ticket to your destination, provided that you have to wait four hours or more. The minimum they will pay is £10 and the maximum is £100.

On domestic flights within the UK you can claim half the cost of your single ticket if you have to hang around for more than two hours as a result of being bumped.

The airline should tell you that you are entitled to this compensation when they break the news that they can't give you the seat you have reserved. They should then either give you the money or a voucher which can later be exchanged for cash.

You can also ask the airline to reimburse you for any reasonable expenses you incur because of the delay. They will pay for phone calls, for instance, and if you have to stay overnight to get a flight next day, they must also pay the hotel bill. But you will have to ask for the money. And don't book the Royal Suite at Claridge's, of course.

Some people do very nicely, thank you, as a result of the airlines' incompetence, but it's not charity all the way.

You have to have checked in on time – AND have a con-firmed reservation, of course. And the airline doesn't owe you anything if your flight is delayed by strikes, weather or mechanical problems. Sorry about that.

Another snag: The denied-boarding compensation scheme only applies to travellers who are bumped from flights at British airports. If you are bumped on a flight returning home, your rights to compensation will depend on where you're coming from.

The US and Australian governments have both passed laws to provide compensation if you're bumped from planes in their countries. Elsewhere you will have to argue for an ex-gratia payment. British Airways say they will probably pay compensation at about the same rate as you'd get in the UK.

Try not to get involved in arguments and threats with stewards, stewardesses or clerks on the check-in counter. They have no real authority to solve disputes and you should demand to speak instead to the Duty Officer, an on-the-spot troubleshooter who is at the airport round-the-clock.

You can always register your protest and wait until later to fight the big battle, of course.

Most airlines have large offices in the capital of every country they operate in. If your complaint is a fairly minor one, take it up with the Customer Relations Department. If that doesn't get you anywhere, write to the Managing Director or Chief Executive at head office.

Your final court of appeal is the Air Transport Users' Committee, recently set up by the Civil Aviation Authority to protect passengers' interests. They have been known to persuade or cajole airlines to dip into their bottomless pockets and pay passengers compensation for unnecessary suffering or loss. Place your troubles on their shoulders if all else fails – it's what they're there for.

WARD'S LAW: Fight the bad flight with all your might.

APPOINTMENTS

Delivery drivers, plumbers, electricians, fitters, decorators, engineers, chimney-sweeps and window-cleaners all have one thing in common. They never turn up when they say they will.

They give you their solemn word they will call on you at 2 pm on Friday, 16 January, and there you are, still waiting for them to arrive, at 3.20 pm on Tuesday, 24 February.

It is estimated that housewives waste more than one

million days every year waiting for repairmen who never turn up. For those who go out to work, the expense and inconvenience of waiting around at home can be even greater.

You may well have wondered if there is some kind of a conspiracy afoot that keeps so many diverse tradesfolk from your home. There is no plot, however. They went round to Mrs Smith's house, instead.

Why Mrs Smith and not you?

Well, when they set off on their calls from the depot that morning, the foreman said: 'Whatever happens today, Harry, even if it means leaving 10 Downing Street until next week, for Christ's sake don't be late for that old cow Mrs Smith. I don't want the old bag on the phone to me every five minutes asking where the hell you are.'

Take a tip from Mrs Smith. INSIST on being given a firm appointment at a fixed time. Your best chance, when this suggestion is vigorously opposed, is to ask for the 'first call' – morning or afternoon. And, like Mrs Smith, when he doesn't turn up on time, don't be afraid to get on the telephone to the depot to report the tardy repair man as a missing person.

WARD'S LAW: Tardy tradesmen can your home a prison make.

ATTRACTING ATTENTION

Some years ago, a South American government was elected, overthrown, the president executed and the new revolutionary leader installed in the palace, all in the time it took me to buy a pair of socks in a Manchester store. Well, nearly.

To many shop assistants and waiters, customers are nothing more than a very irritating interruption to a rather good book. So unless you don't mind spending five years of your waking life standing around in shops, pubs and res-

taurants waiting to be served, it's up to you to *make* them notice you.

This is how you do it:

IN RESTAURANTS: If the waiter won't come to the customer, take the customer to the waiter. Walk up to him slowly and confidently and confront him with your order. It's a public challenge to his professionalism, not to mention the infringement of his territorial rights, and with a bit of luck he won't let it happen again.

If it's the bill you're waiting for, get up to go. The waiter will meet you with it at the door.

IN SHOPS: Accidently lean against a display of 240 tins of baked beans. If there's nothing around you can upset, such as in a furniture showroom, sit down on the most expensive piece in the shop. When the manager comes to tell you off, tell him you had been waiting so long to be served that you thought you were going to faint.

WARD'S LAW: A castaway on a desert island doesn't wave a hankie to attract attention. He lights a fire.

BANKS

Most people have the same kind of relationship with their bank manager as they do with God. They live in awe of him, feel that he is watching everything they do, and every night they pray that he will forgive them their sins and give them their daily bread.

Far from being gods, bank managers are actually no more than junior under-gods in banking circles, let alone the heavenly hierarchy. They have to answer primarily to their local head office and ultimately to the General Manager at head office in London.

I've always owed my bank manager too much money to dare to complain about him, but if I wanted to put the screws on him I would do one of three things, depending on how much he had upset me.

1. I would threaten (a) to take away my account, and (b) to write a letter to the District Manager at the local head office telling him why I had done so. (Banks are very sensitive about losing even the smallest customer, so this ought to bring all but the stroppiest bank manager to heel.)

2. I would actually write to the District Manager. (Anyone at your bank will tell you who – and where – he is.)

3. I would by-pass them all and write straight to the bigwigs, the General Managers at the bank's head office in London.

Banks, their managers, and their computers make many mistakes, but about the worst thing they can do is bounce a cheque when you actually have money in your current or a deposit account to cover the cheque. By returning your cheque with those dreaded words, 'Refer to Drawer', they are in fact libelling you. Mr Geoffrey Downham, a property dealer, sued Giro, the Post Office's national banking system, for doing just that, and was awarded damages against them.

If one of your cheques is bounced in similar circumstances, you should see a solicitor and insist that the bank writes an explanatory letter of apology to the person to whom the cheque was payable.

Personally, I think the trouble with bank managers is not so much how to complain about them but how to get money out of them. This is a subject I know a great deal about and I have a sizeable overdraft to prove it. This is how it is done.

First of all you have to find some kind of a hold over him to blackmail him with. This shouldn't be too difficult. All you have to do is wait until he sends you someone else's bank statement by mistake.

Ring him up and tell him you'll send it on to the customer yourself, with a note explaining how you came to have it.

When, trying to conceal the panic in his voice, he asks you to let *him* have it back, say you quite understand and would hate to embarrass him by letting the other customer know about his slip-up.

He now owes you a favour – good for a couple of hundred quid overdraft any time – and you still hold an ace card of being able to threaten to rat on him to the other customer if it ever came to a showdown.

You can also cash in on other mistakes the bank makes – they may be made by a clerk or a computer, but ultimately they reflect on the manager. A few years ago my bank credited my account with £29,000 belonging to another customer. To this day my bank manager's face goes the colour of his shirt every time I mention it.

The way has now been cleared to presenting your

FOR WHAT MY BANK WILL EVENTUALLY PAY FOR MAY THE LORD MAKE US TRULY THANKFUL...

AMEN!

'convincing argument' to borrow money. However dire the threat you hold over them, bank managers are on the whole disinclined to advance large sums of cash for a dead cert in the 2.30 at Doncaster. On the other hand, rotting gutters, roof repairs, washroom extensions and essential office equipment are a winner every time.

What you mustn't do is let him know you're going to spend it on something he wants but hasn't got, such as a boat. Ask for a colour telly before he's got one and you'll be bounced out of the bank faster than your cheques.

A lot of the customers make the mistake of believing that the amount they are allowed to borrow is fixed according to their salary.

This is not the case at all. It is the bank manager's salary that decides how much you will get. Bank managers rarely lend a sum exceeding half their own salary and then, sadists that they are, fix the repayments at a sum that brings your income to less than one half of theirs.

It's also worth remembering that when a bank manager says No, he means it. A friend of mine took his bank manager out to lunch some time ago to discuss a large loan. The manager said No. At the end of the meal my friend paid by cheque. The cheque bounced.

WARD'S LAW: Banks are only in it for the money.

BLACK LISTS

Before lending you money or giving you credit, most firms will take the wise precaution of checking you out with a credit-reference agency. Are you a person of substance? Do you pay your debts? You can't blame them for wanting to know.

If you have a bad record for repaying debts, your name is quite likely to be among the many hundreds of thousands on the agencies' black lists. When the shop or finance company is given the details from your file, you will suffer the humiliation of being shown the door.

But even if you DON'T have a bad record, it's possible that some bureaucratic bungle has put your name in the hall of shame.

Only YOU know whether you deserve to be blacked, so if you feel an injustice has been done – or for that matter even if you feel an injustice *hasn't* been done – you are entitled to see the credit agency's file on you. This is your right under the Consumer Credit Act.

If a shop or finance company turns down your application for credit, ask them if they have consulted an agency. They are obliged to reply truthfully and to tell you the name of the agency. You should then write to the agency, enclosing a 25p fee, asking for a copy of any file they have on you. Under the Act, they have to do this.

If the file is wrong, you can ask the agency to correct it. If they decline to do so, you can still write a note of correction up to 200 words long which the agency must then attach to your file and give to anyone who makes further enquiries

about your credit-worthiness. If the agency fails to do this or doesn't reply, you should ask the Director-General of Fair Trading to help.

Motivated by nothing more than idle curiosity, you might be interested to know what, if anything, these agencies have got on you, anyway. Two of the biggest are the United Association for Protection of Trade at Zodiac House, 163 London Road, Croydon, Surrey; and Credit Data Ltd, at Markham House, Markham Road, Chesterfield, Derbyshire. Drop them a line – and 25p – and if they've got anything on you, I bet you won't be able to put it down.

Personally, I don't see why black lists should be a one-sided business. Why, I often ask myself, aren't there similar black lists of firms, shops, restaurants, etc., who are equally bad risks to the unsuspecting customers who patronize them?

For a small annual subscription you would be able to find out whether an electrician is likely to turn up when he says he will, or whether an HP company is run by financiers or a gang of extortionists.

In the absence of any such public service I have compiled over the years my own black list of 'offenders'. New names are added to it daily, with the result that I will soon either have to revise it drastically or go and live in another country.

It's not easy to get on my black list, but a surprising number of establishments have managed. Once they are on it there is no appeal and the boycott is operated ruthlessly.

I suppose there are more restaurants than anything else on the list. Generally speaking poisonous food is not sufficient reason to bring in a total boycott. But if the food is bad, the service poor *and* the head waiter follows me to my car with an empty plate in his hand complaining that I haven't left a tip, then on the list it goes.

One quick way for a firm to get on my black list is to refuse to take a cheque when they know I've done business with them before. Anyone I suspect has taken me for a ride gets on the black list pretty fast, too.

Depriving errant firms of your money is a satisfying business, but at times it takes a lot of self-discipline to observe it. There is a distinct possibility, for instance, that there will soon be nowhere I can eat out in central London.

Keep a black list, observe it ruthlessly, and exchange names with friends who keep one, too. No firm can afford to be on *too* many people's black lists.

WARD'S LAW: Ban the bum.

BRITISH RAIL

Who is the chap in charge?

Nothing could be more simple. All you have to remember is that a Railman is junior to a Leading Railman, who is junior to a Senior Railman, who is junior to a Charge Man, who is junior to a Station Supervisor, who is junior to a Station Manager, who is junior to an Assistant Area Manager, who is junior to an Area Manager, who is junior to a Divisional Manager, who is junior to a Chief Passenger Manager, who is junior to the Assistant General Manager, who is junior to the General Manager, who is junior to the Chief Executive of the British Railways Board, who is junior to the Chairman of the British Railways Board, who is junior to . . .

The problem is knowing which junior to grab by the short and curlies when something goes wrong.

To understand the enormous obstacles facing a dissatisfied passenger, you have to imagine British Rail as an enormous chess board with, say, two thousand squares. There is no point whatsoever in blaming the chap in charge of square 247 for something that happened in square 1832, because you – and the blame – will simply be shunted from one square to the next until you finally give up out of boredom, exhaustion or old age.

How do you find the right square?

The railway network is divided into five regions – London-Midland, Southern, Western, Eastern, and Scottish. Each region is headed by a General Manager who has to answer to the top brass, the British Railways Board. Under him are a Chief Passenger Manager and up to ten Divisional

Managers. Each Divisional Manager has under him perhaps a dozen Area Managers.

Let's take a common enough occurrence. Say your train from King's Cross to Newcastle arrives ninety minutes late, causing you to miss a connection and spend the night in a hotel in Newcastle.

From whom in the Eastern Region do you attempt to extract your hotel expenses? The Divisional Manager (London, King's Cross) from where the train started? The Divisional Manager (Newcastle) where the train arrived late? Or the Divisional Manager (Doncaster) where the train sat outside a tunnel for forty minutes?

In a situation like this the best bet is to pin the blame on the man in charge of all three Divisional Managers – the General Manager whose name and address can be found in the front of the timetable for that particular region. (In this particular case, the General Manager of the Eastern Region, who is in York.)

Complaints about stations or station staff, on the other hand, should be sent to the 'Area Manager' who has responsibility for that particular station. He's the bloke who puts on his tails and topper to shake hands with the Queen when the Royal Train leaves or arrives at his station and is the equivalent of what we all know as Station Masters.

He will probably try to pass your complaint down the line to an Assistant Area Manager or a Senior Station Supervisor. If you're not satisfied with the reply you get, leap-frog them all and take your complaint to the Divisional Manager, whose name can also be found in front of the timetable.

Failing that, there's always the General Manager. But if you still don't get anywhere there, then you'll have to take it right to the top, the British Railways Board.

The man who, in the end, carries the can for everything that goes wrong – including your parrot's cage that has gone missing somewhere between Haverfordwest and Moreton-in-

Marsh – is the Chairman, Sir Peter Parker at the time of going to press. Sir Peter has been rash enough to place on record that he welcomes complaints from passengers. Try not to disappoint him.

How do you get through to Train Enquiries when the line is always engaged or no one ever answers?

Life, alas, isn't long enough for we mortals to spend on the phone trying to get through to Train Enquiries. It's quicker to walk to your destination.

There IS a way of finding out train times by phone, however. Look up the number of the station itself – NOT the Train Enquiries number listed in the telephone book – and call it.

Switchboard staff have strict orders to refer all enquiries about train times to the Enquiries number, so *do not yet reveal the reason for your call*.

Instead, ask to speak to the Area Manager's office and say you wish to make a complaint.

When you get through, say you wish to complain about the Train Enquiries service and tell him how long you've been trying to get through to the number.

He will apologize and explain that it's because of the Christmas rush, or because they're short-staffed, or it's the holiday period, or it's always like this on Tuesday mornings.

Sound understanding about his problems, but tell him that you also have problems, the most pressing of which is the time of the next train to Little Nuttingford.

He may well then volunteer this information, but if he doesn't, then ask him for it. He will have all the relevant timetables in front of him, after all.

If he declines to help you, referring you back to the eternally unobtainable Enquiries number, ask for his name and position and tell him you will report his unhelpfulness at 'Divisional Manager level' unless he can put you through to someone who does know.

A word of warning about complaining about anything to do with BR on the telephone: brave and clever men have been turned into gibbering idiots trying to find the right person to help them with their particular problem. This is because BR appears to have been organized with a view to confusing even its own staff.

The difficulty is this: if you dial the number that is in the telephone book for, say, Victoria Station, you will in fact get through to the main Southern Region switchboard at Waterloo, although you won't know it.

When you then ask to speak to the 'Area Manager' – a reasonable enough request, you might think – the switchboard girl will have before her a list of perhaps twenty area managers, nineteen of whom will be the wrong person for your problem. So when you have found your man, always extract a name and a title if you ever want to find him again.

What about complaints about dining cars and buffet cars – or, more often than not, the absence of them?

These should be addressed to the Regional Train Catering Manager at the station that the train started out from.

Curling sandwiches in the station buffet, however, should be brought to the attention of the Station Catering Manager at British Transport Hotels Ltd.

What is the BR Book of Rules and Regulations and would I like it?

The Railman's bible is a hefty eighty-page tome called the British Rail Book of Rules and Regulations. In it lies the answer to every conceivable eventuality that could arise on the railways, and a few inconceivable eventualities, too.

Any railwayman who has taken the trouble to memorize page fourteen knows exactly what to do when confronted with a nurseryman travelling with sixty pounds of daffodil bulbs, a folding canoe, an uncaged parrot and a harp 4ft 7in tall.

(*For the disbelieving: as he's a nurseryman he can carry*

his bulbs free; as his canoe collapses, that is free, too; the parrot will have to go in a cage and costs a child's fare; his harp is an inch too high to be carried free so he has to have a child's ticket for that, too. All this, of course, is supposing that he isn't travelling on an excursion ticket, etc., when a different set of rules and regulations applies.)

The R and R are available for inspection (or ought to be) at every ticket office, where there is also a shortened, expurgated version more suitable for public consumption.

Not all railmen are familiar with its contents, so if you're in any doubt it's as well to have a look at the book at the enquiry office – you could save yourself a few quid.

You could also save yourself an argument or two. A friend was charged six bob by a railway lost property office for feeding his lost budgie for two days. He protested that the bird didn't eat that much food in a year.

He should have saved his breath and paid up straight away. It's all in the Book of Rules and Regulations.

If railwaymen can go on strike in protest against conditions, why shouldn't the passengers?

They can and they do. And very effective a sit-in by passengers is, too.

Businessman Mr John Wright of Effingham was a passenger one night on the 8.02 pm from Waterloo to Guildford, via Effingham Junction.

When the train arrived at Wimbledon Mr Wright saw another train to Effingham pull out, but he stayed put because his train was going to Effingham.

The guard then announced that Mr Wright's train was being taken out of service and that there would be no more trains to Effingham that night.

Everyone got out. Mr Wright stayed put.

This is what happened, in Mr Wright's own words:

'There were no offers of alternative transport, so I told them that I was not prepared to get out.

'I asked to see the station master. Another gentleman came along and there was some talk of calling the police. I said, "Good, go ahead and call them."

'By this time other passengers had gained some confidence and were back on the train with me.

'After about an hour and ten minutes a relief driver arrived and we eventually got to Effingham Junction at about 10 o'clock.'

Another passenger told newsmen who covered this fine display of commuter courage: 'Mr Wright was a real champion. If it hadn't been for him we would have been stranded the night at Wimbledon as far as Southern Region were concerned.'

Can the Transport Users' Consultative Committees help a passenger in distress?

Yes, but it's probably best to go it alone at first. If it looks like you're going to have a full-scale battle with BR bring them in on your side by all means. You will find the address posted up somewhere near the booking office, but if you can't find it, the Enquiry office will know.

Consultative committees do a lot of valuable work beating out revised timetables and train schedules with British Rail, and they are the people to get in touch with if your complaint is about a service rather than a particular incident.

Rail travel is an expensive commodity these days and if you feel you have not had your money's worth, don't hesitate to say so. You are perfectly entitled to claim all or a proportion of your fare back if the service did not reach the standards you might reasonably expect it to. British Rail will, and often do, pay out compensation to dissatisfied travellers, though they try not to advertise this.

Industrial action by BR staff is no excuse – it's the Railway Board's problem, not yours – and you should demand a proportionate refund of your ticket money, or an extension of your season ticket if you have been prevented from travelling by go-slows, strikes, etc.

WARD'S LAW: It's not the porter's fault your train is late.

BUILDERS

I feel like a doctor who says to a sick patient, 'You should never have caught it. There's nowt I can do, so I'll be off now.' But that's rather how it is with builders, I'm afraid.

There are so many bad builders, so many builders who go bankrupt at the drop of a brick, that prevention is far surer than any cure.

How you deal with builders depends on whether you are buying a new home or paying for alterations to an existing one.

NEW HOMES

Builders are in a hurry to get houses built to make a quick profit. You're in a hurry to get a roof over your head before someone else gets it.

In the rush, you're both likely to get careless – only you're the one who pays for his mistakes.

So unless you want to end up mortgaged to the hilt, living in a shored-up ruin, the first thing you must do is make sure he is a good builder.

What else has he built and is it still standing? How long has he been in business? What do people living in some of the other places he's built have to say about them? Knock on a few doors if necessary.

Rule two is don't buy a new house unless it is covered by the National House-Building Council guarantee. It's doubtful if you would be able to get a mortgage for one that isn't, anyway.

What is the NHBC?

It's an independent non-profit-making organization that guarantees new houses built by member builders for up to ten years. The system doesn't work quite as wonderfully as it sounds, but it's a lot better than shutting your eyes and taking pot luck.

What happens is this: builders registered with NHBC have to tell the Council when they are about to start building a house. An inspector visits the site every three weeks or so during construction to make sure the builders are actually putting cement between the bricks, etc. If the inspector finds defects, the builder has to put them right.

When a building is completed, an inspector makes a final inspection and if it doesn't fall down when he leans against it, the house gets a ten-year guarantee certificate.

This means that the builder has to put right all defects free for the first two years and major constructional faults for the next eight.

If the builder disputes these faults, there's an arbitration procedure. If the builder goes bankrupt, the NHBC will pay for another builder to put the place right for you.

Bad builders are struck off the register, and as this means

virtual blacklisting by building societies and solicitors, it's a fairly effective deterrent.

The snag is the 'major structural defects' bit. A lot can go wrong with a house without the roof blowing off or the whole thing disappearing into a hole in the ground, and you could easily find yourself, after the two-year minor-defects guarantee expires, having to spend several hundred pounds replastering walls, eliminating rising damp, or re-tiling the roof to keep the rain out.

If this happens and the builder declines responsibility, you should certainly do battle with the NHBC anyway, and failing that, have a private survey done with a view to suing the builder.

A lot of new home-owners fall out with the NHBC over differences of opinion over acceptable standards of workmanship. It seems that sloping walls and uneven plastering are the rule rather than the exception these days and many house-buyers have been horrified to find that, having insisted on having all their walls re-plastered, a worse job was done second time round.

If in doubt, get a second opinion from your own surveyor.

And a warning to second owners of new houses: don't be lulled into a false sense of security by the ten-year guarantee you inherit from the previous owners.

A condition of the guarantee is that faults are reported as soon as possible. If the previous owner failed to do this – as well he might have, knowing he was moving away – you could find yourself bankrupted by out-of-guarantee repairs. The solution is to have a survey done before buying.

Building alterations

The NHBC won't guarantee or inspect any building work that doesn't involve new homes, so you must exercise a fox-like caution. All the bad things you have heard about builders are true – and there are worse to come. Here are a few tips which will save your money even if they don't save your marriage.

· DON'T engage any builder until he has given you at least two references from people like yourself who have had work done by him. Visit them at home and inspect the builder's standard of workmanship yourself.

DON'T employ fly-by-night cowboys. They'll bodge the job and when the wall falls down, you'll never know where to find them.

DO employ a private surveyor if you are spending more than £2,000 or if the work necessitates architect's plans.

ALWAYS make sure the builder is further ahead with the work than you are with the payments. Retain five or ten per cent of the total price for an agreed period after the work has been completed. Bad workmanship can take time to reveal itself and this is your only insurance.

HOPE for the worst and expect only a catastrophe. You won't get any surprises.

WARD'S LAW: An Englishman's home is his ruination.

BUREAUCRATS

The first thing you have to realize about bureaucrats is that in the Civil Service no one gets paid to make decisions.

The second thing is that everything is done by the rule-book.

Nothing that you or I do, beg, promise or threaten is going to change that, and, until you accept this, you haven't a hope of surviving the System – let alone beating it.

To gain insight into the lugubrious workings of the Civil-Service mind you only have to read some of the bumph that comes out of Whitehall. You will notice from any letters you have received from Government departments, for instance, that there is a complete reluctance on the part of the writer ever to commit himself to an opinion.

He's *inclined to take the view that* . . . or he passes the buck completely by saying that he has been *advised that* . . . He doesn't ever permit himself the luxury of *thinking*.

No one ever says sorry. They say, *it is regretted that* . . . No one ever says 'No'. They say that *your request has unfortunately received a negative response*. Conditions are never good. They're *not unfavourable*. When a project is cocked up, the plans *unfortunately failed to materialize*.

When it's suddenly Your Turn Next at the Social Security counter, it can all be very overwhelming. But it needn't be when you know your enemy and are prepared to play the game by his rules.

Quite contrary to the 'faceless' image that they have acquired, civil servants are in fact more vulnerable to criticism and attack than any other professional group.

How?

Most civil servants are extremely badly paid and have been dumped into departments they never wanted to work in. Their only hope is that the next round of promotions will bring them a transfer and more money. Their only fear is that something will happen to block this promotion.

In true Civil-Service tradition, detailed records are kept of all Government employees and every black mark against them is carefully noted down. Even allegations which are proved to be totally unfounded are recorded.

In a profession that thrives on its lack of controversy, any kind of a row therefore is a threat to a civil servant's promotion.

It is for this reason that no bureaucrat ever sticks his neck out, and can you blame him? He won't even volunteer an opinion about the weather. If he is in any doubt about whether it is an overcast day or a moderate day, he will refer the matter to a higher level or another department.

To you and me it smacks of bloody-minded unhelpfulness. It isn't. It's doing everything by the book.

How can you beat the book?

Unfortunately you have to know your rights before you get tangled up in the Civil-Service machine. No one is going to give you form P46B unless you ask for it. No one is going to tell you that you're eligible for a grant or a rebate unless you apply for it.

Arm yourself with all the facts and information you need to know by visiting a Citizens' Advice Bureau beforehand.

DON'T be bullied or intimidated by a self-important counter-clerk. If you don't know how to fill in a form – ask him to help you. That's what he's there for. If you can't understand something – don't be afraid to ask someone to translate it from gobbledegook for you.

DON'T take no for an answer. You are entitled to know the name of the person you are talking to, and to ask to be referred to someone of a more senior rank. If you're told they're busy, say you'll wait – and sit it out if you have to.

DON'T be fobbed off with the old excuse about your letter or file being mislaid. Every letter and even telephone calls received by Government departments have to be scrupulously recorded, and every file signed for before being taken out. The loss of a file is tantamount to arson or murder in the Civil Service and you should threaten to pursue this at the highest level. Don't worry. It will soon be 'found'.

BE POLITE, but always firm. Insist that unless they find a solution to your problem you will take it up with your MP and complain about the lack of assistance you have received.

If you're writing a letter of complaint, always put on the bottom, 'Copy to Mr –, MP', even if you don't send him a copy. It should help to get things moving that little bit faster.

Government departments are *not*, as some people seem to think, above the law. In any civilized country they have to obey the law of the land as rigidly as we do. Ask ex-President Nixon.

Finally, remember that all the unkind stories you've ever heard about the bureaucrats are probably true. Especially, I suspect, the one about the Minister who asked his Parliamentary secretary, 'How many civil servants work in Whitehall, Rogers?'

Back came the answer: 'About one in three, sir.'

WARD'S LAW: Pick your target and make his life a misery.

BUSES

Most bus companies would be doing a fine job if they were in the cattle transportation business instead of running a bus service for humans.

Cattle and sheep are happy to graze by the roadside for hours on end waiting for their transport to arrive, they never complain about overcrowded or dirty conditions, and stragglers and ditherers can be hurried aboard with a sharp prod up the backside.

But with human loads, bus companies and their herdsmen are often less than tactful or efficient, and you may find you have to remind them that you are not an Aberdeen Angus or a black-face Cheviot.

There are more than a hundred different bus companies operating in Britain. A third of them are run by the State-owned National Bus Company. Of the rest, a few are privately owned, others are controlled by local councils. Some, like London Transport, don't seem to be run by anyone. We'll start with them.

LONDON TRANSPORT

The London Transport Executive, as it is called, is in charge of the day-to-day running of all red buses and Tubes in the London area. If you have any complaints or suggestions about routes, services or bloody-minded bus conductors you should write to the Public Relations Officer, who is their troubleshooter and Chief Fobber-Off.

He won't however fob you off quite so quickly if you write in bold letters at the top of your letter: Copy to

41

Mr Ian G. McLeod, Chairman, London Transport Passengers Committee and Mr –, MP (your local member).

Unless you are planning a full-scale battle with London Transport you don't actually have to bother to send these people a copy, it's just a tactical precaution to keep the Chief Fobber-Off on his toes.

If you're not satisfied with the Chief Fobber-Off's reply you can do one of two things.

> 1. *Write to the London Transport Passengers Committee, an independent body set up to pursue passengers' grievances with LT, and let them fight it out for you. OR –*
> 2. *Take it up at a higher level – with the Chairman of London Transport, Mr Ralph Bennett. But don't let him bounce you back to the Chief Fobber-Off.*

THE NATIONAL BUS COMPANY

This is Britain's largest bus company, with 18,000 vehicles and more than 65,000 staff. It owns small companies with unlikely-sounding names, such as The Potteries Motor Traction Company, as well as the bigger and better-known services like the Greenline London Country Bus Service.

There are too many to list here, but many of their buses can be identified by the company's insignia, a double-headed arrow tip.

The headquarters of the company is in London. But for administrative reasons they have divided the country into four regions – South-East, Northern, Midlands and West, and Wales and the Marches – each with a Regional Director in charge.

(You'll find the addresses of all four Regional Directors at the back of this book, but first check with the bus company to make sure which region it's in, if you're in any doubt.)

Each Regional Director controls a number of operating

companies. At the head of each operating bus company is a General Manager.

The only exceptions to this power structure are:

1. The London Country Bus Services (Green Line), which have a Managing Director in charge at the head office in Lesbourne Road, Reigate, Surrey, and:
2. The coaching subsidiaries that trade under the name National Travel (NBC) Ltd. There are four of these: West, East, South-West and London, with a General Manager in charge of each. (The London region only handles Continental coach services and excursions.) They all answer ultimately to: The Director of Coaching, Mr Robert G. Roberts, who can be tracked down to this address: National Travel (NBC) Ltd, Victoria Coach Station, London SW1.

So who is the best person to go to with your ear-bashing?

If it's a fairly minor complaint, such as a bloody-minded bus conductor, late running, etc., take it up with the General Manager of the bus company. He's the man on the spot after all. But write at the top of the letter, 'Copy to Regional Director', just so that he knows he's not dealing with an idiot.

If that doesn't get you anywhere, or you wish to draw your plight to the attention of someone even higher up, write to the Regional Director and send a copy to the Chairman in London.

The next stop after that is a direct attack on head office in London. The Chairman is Lord Shepherd. His number two at the office is Mr Robert Brook.

You might bear in mind when writing to them however that probably neither of them travels to work by bus.

CORPORATION-RUN BUS SERVICES

As with all bureaucratic-minded organizations, there's no point in beating about the bush. Write to the Transport

Manager and indicate that a copy has been sent to the Chairman of the Transport Committee.

If that doesn't get you anywhere, write to the Chairman of the Transport Committee and ask your local councillor if he can help out. He will be only too happy to make a hero of himself in the local paper by helping you out.

WARD'S LAW: All fair for all fares, please.

CAR DEALERS AND GARAGES

For most of us, a car is the second greatest single expense after our home. But while a house or a flat appreciates all the time, a car goes down in value every day. You can practically see it happening. To prevent it becoming an even bigger financial burden, you have to exercise the greatest vigilance.

NEW CARS

Before the introduction of the Supply of Goods (Implied Terms) Act in 1973, the new car buyer had to rely on a rather unfavourable warranty and the goodwill of the manufacturers if anything went wrong with his new toy.

The makers promised to replace defective parts during the warranty period, but *you* had to pay the labour charges. It meant that the owner of a new car might have to spend £50 to have an engine stripped down – to replace a defective washer, price 1p, generously donated by the makers. But under the new Act, they have to pay the labour charges, too.

The Act is a real godsend for the hard-pressed motorist, in fact. If his new car is off the road while a manufacturing defect is being rectified, the dealer has to lend him another car or pay for the hire of another car.

Another bonus: dealers can't turn round and plead immunity because the warranty mileage or time-limit has been exceeded. *So long as you can prove that the failure of a component was due to a manufacturing defect, you can, in theory, make a claim up to six years after you bought it.*

This doesn't mean that every new car carries a six-year guarantee, but it is a blessing to the motorist who is told that his three-month-old car needs a new gearbox but is just out of warranty because it has 13,000 miles on the clock.

It is the dealer – *not* the manufacturer – who carries this legal burden, so don't let the dealer pass the buck by suggesting that you take your fight to the manufacturer yourself. That's his job.

What about rogue cars?

In the past, motor manufacturers have always refused to admit that such cars exist. They would respray a new car, fit a new engine and gearbox, and rebuild the suspension four times no matter what the cost. But they would never, however much bad publicity it brought them, replace the car, for fear of setting a precedent.

Their stubbornness led to some colourful protests by the enraged owners of new 'rogue' cars. Engineer Keith Greatrex blocked the main entrance to the British Leyland factory at Longbridge until someone came out to see about his troublesome Austin Maxi.

Schoolmaster Ian Newton pasted the windows of his Morris 1100 with notices listing all its faults. Another car owner went so far as to set fire to his car outside the Vauxhall factory.

It's still virtually unknown for a manufacturer to replace a 'rogue' car. But, thanks to the law it should be possible to recover the purchase price.

But before you take this drastic step, write to the manufacturers pressing them to supply your dealer with a replacement. Send a copy of the letter to the Society of Motor Manufacturers asking them to pursue your case.

If that fails, then you will just have to revoke the sale, return the car to the dealer, and sue under the Sale of Goods Act, which says that goods have to be 'of merchantable quality' and 'fit for the purpose for which they are intended'.

That is what barrister Michael Spencer did, winning a significant victory for us all.

He bought a new Triumph which was plagued with defect after defect. His patience exhausted, he chucked it back at the dealer he bought it from and demanded a new car. They refused, offering instead to have another go at putting it right.

Mr Spencer sued the garage, claiming that the car was not of merchantable quality – and won.

SECOND-HAND CARS

There's an old common-law maxim that says, 'Let the buyer beware', and it applies to nothing more than to second-hand cars. When you buy a second-hand car, the chances are you are taking on someone else's troubles.

Prevention is easier and cheaper than litigation, so find out what you're buying by getting an AA or RAC engineer's report if you're a member. You can protect yourself further by buying the car from a reputable dealer who will give you a guarantee that will be honoured.

Take along a friend as a witness: if the seller – trade or private – assures you that it would be a suitable vehicle for your proposed safari to Afghanistan, then you have a water-tight case of misrepresentation when the engine drops out at the end of the street.

It's an offence under the Trade Descriptions Act to turn a car mileometer back, by the way.

But even with all the care in the world, you can still come a cropper over a second-hand car.

If things *do* go wrong, don't go screaming and stamping about the showroom threatening lawsuits and demanding your rights. Speak or write to the Managing Director of the company telling him calmly what has happened and what you expect him to do about it.

If that doesn't work – and, unless you are dealing with a veritable saint it probably won't – then your only hope is that the dealer is a member of the Motor Agents' Association, to which more than 14,500 garages and dealers belong.

The Association acts as an independent trouble-shooting referee in disputes between motor agents and their customers. It is a Mecca of unhappy motoring tales.

Write to their Conciliation Service giving all the relevant details, and they will send you back a leaflet explaining the rules and a complaints form that you must fill in. (Don't groan, it isn't as bad as some I've seen.) The very intervention of the MAA might miraculously bring about a compromise settlement. Or the Association may want an independent engineer's examination of the car, which they will pay for.

But if they can't settle the dispute amicably, you can ask for the claim to go to arbitration. It costs £8.10, which is returned if you win, and the arbitrator's decision is legally binding on both parties.

SERVICING AND REPAIRS

A few years ago I was driving up the A1 when I heard a tinkling noise coming from the engine. Was it the end of a big end? A broken half-shaft? Loose tappets, perhaps?

Knowing nothing whatsoever about the mysterious workings of the internal combustion engine, I pulled into a lay-by and stopped an AA patrol.

The AA man poked about under the bonnet for a few minutes. Then he asked: 'Have you by any chance had this car serviced recently, sir?'

'Yes, as a matter of fact I picked it up from the garage only this morning.'

'I think I've found what the trouble is,' he said. 'It's a cup of tea.'

He produced a large mug that had been delicately balanced on the battery.

Well, that's what happens when you let people muck about with your car. They adjust the brake shoes and two days later the back window falls out. Funny how there was nothing wrong with it until they started fiddling around with those brakes.

The trouble is that if, like me, you haven't the slightest idea what goes on under a car bonnet, you can't very well argue when the foreman tells you: 'Bad news, I'm afraid. The overhead camshaft gasket is hitting the vacuum pump release valve.'

'Oh dear, is it?' you say, not having the foggiest what he's talking about. 'Is that going to be very expensive?'

The answer to all servicing problems therefore is to take a course in motor engineering at your local college of further education and do it yourself.

The next best thing is to find a good garage and stick with it. How can you tell if a garage is good? Have a look around the workshop and apply the restaurant kitchen principle to it. Does it look tidy? Are the workmen and the work benches reasonably clean and orderly?

The biggest question-mark is always *has the work I have paid for been done?*

If you don't know about cars, it's almost impossible to know for sure. But if you have spent a lot of money and you have your doubts, it would be worth spending a tenner to get a second opinion from another garage or an AA or RAC engineer.

Always ask for a detailed break-down of the work done to your car, so that if there is a dispute, you can see where the money is supposed to have gone.

Always ask the garage – in writing – to keep defective parts if you plan to make a claim on the manufacturer. It's not enough to say that a replacement rear axle snapped after only 250 miles. The makers will want to see it to find out why. No axle, no pay-out.

The Motor Agents' Association also sort out punch-ups over repairs in exactly the same way as they settle second-hand car disputes. Write to their Conciliation Service.

What should you do if you dispute a bill, but the garage won't release your car until you have paid in full?

It is unlikely that the garage would be daft enough to take a cheque which you could then stop after you have your car back. So insist on seeing an executive about the disputed bill – the works foreman or the Service Director have no real authority in these matters once the bill has gone through.

If the garage is a member of the MAA suggest that you pay at least some of the disputed bill, get your car back, and agree to abide by the MAA's decision over the unpaid items. You'll probably find they will make you an offer without having to bring the MAA into it.

WARD'S LAW: Don't let your car drive you mad.

CAR PARKS

Nearly all car parks and garages try to protect themselves with a long list of 'terms and conditions' that, when translated, mean: heads we win, tails you lose.

But, with a bit of luck, when you return to collect your car and discover that it has been lost, stolen, damaged, broken into, overrun by rats, sprayed with acid or used for machine-gun practice, the car-park management may not be able to wriggle out of its responsibilities.

Regardless of what the terms and conditions say, the Unfair Contract Terms Act makes them liable for loss or damage if they haven't taken *reasonable* steps to look after your car.

Just what is 'reasonable' may, ultimately, be up to a court to decide, but the Act defines negligence as any lack of proper skill or care. (See 'Small Print'.)

Don't expect car park managements to give in without a fight. They have been dodging their responsibilities for so many years now they still can't get used to the new rules.

WARD'S LAW: Don't abandon hope all ye who enter car parks.

CHEQUES

The customer who pays by cheque holds an ace bargaining card. Cheques usually take two days before they reach your bank and are paid, two valuable days in which you may discover you've been sold a pup in time to stop the cheque.

Withholding payment obviously gives you valuable bargaining power when you take the goods (or repaired goods) back to the shop. Instead of being on the defensive, fighting to get your money back or your money's worth, the onus is on them to satisfy *you*.

Stopping a cheque is not a step to take lightly since you are in effect fraudulently reneging on your promise to pay, but when you are dealing with a slippery rogue, it's your only certain protection. In the case of a disputed repair bill, it's often the only way to recover what is yours.

To stop a cheque all you have to do is ring your bank and tell them the number of the cheque, to whom it is payable, and the amount it is for. Do not delay, because a villain might ask his bank to 'special' your cheque – i.e. rush through payment in less than twenty-four hours.

You can't however stop a cheque that has been presented with a bank card that guarantees payment of a cheque up to £50.

But there is also another way in which you can use a cheque as a weapon in your complainer's armoury. Cheques, unlike letters of complaint, are always read carefully by those to whom you present them. The cheque therefore makes a suitable medium for you to record your displeasure.

The manager of Lloyds Bank at Richmond, Surrey,

reported a cheque going through his books that was inscribed thus:

'Please pay the H – Hotel, £12.55 for a dreadful meal served extraordinarily slowly.'

WARD'S LAW: You can't stop a £5 note.

CINEMAS

The cinema manager is a familiar figure to us all. He stands there, hands behind his back, oozing smugness, in the warmth and shelter of his foyer while we, his customers, jostle for queuing positions in the pouring rain outside.

When his cinema is showing a successful film, such as the latest James Bond epic, he becomes even more like his hero, Captain Queeg in *The Caine Mutiny*.

He orders his henchmen out to keep the rabble – that's us – in line. He shouts, 'Queuing All Prices!' at every new arrival. He barks at customers to have their money ready. He bars entrances, takes the telephone off the hook so that callers – that's us, too – don't slow the flow of money into his tills. And when all the seats in the house are sold, he has great pleasure in announcing to the next person in the queue that they will have to come back tomorrow.

You would never guess from the way a cinema manager conducts himself that he has any superiors, but indeed he has.

Most of Britain's 1,500 cinemas are owned by four or five big groups, and the managers are just cogs in very big wheels. They are answerable to Area Managers, who in turn have General Managers above them at head office.

If you found something disagreeable about the treatment you received at the cinema, you should speak to the manager about it at the time. Make sure it *is* the manager you speak to and not just an assistant manager behaving like one.

If the manager isn't around, write to him. His name will probably be on display in the foyer (most of them enjoy a bit of star billing), but if not, someone at the box office will tell you.

It could be, of course, that you will find his explanation unsatisfactory or that it is about the manager himself that you wish to complain, in which case you will have to find out which group runs the cinema.

All Odeons and Gaumonts are owned by Rank Leisure Services in London who have an Operations Controller (Theatres) in overall charge of their cinemas. There is also a West End Controller who is responsible for the West End cinemas in London.

The EMI Cinemas and Leisure Group own all ABC cinemas and a few others besides. The man to write to there is the General Manager, who hangs out in London.

In Scotland a chain of cinemas under various names is run by Caledonian. A letter to the General Manager (Cinemas) should reach the right person, but better still, write to the Managing Director and let him sort it out.

If you are unsure of what group a cinema belongs to you are perfectly entitled to ask at the cinema. The manager, wishing to keep his nose clean, may be evasive about it, but you should persist. You could always kid him that you're going to write a letter of praise, in which case he'll probably give you a stamped, addressed envelope.

What will be the outcome?

A letter of apology for your spoiled evening; perhaps two free tickets for another programme there; the satisfaction of getting a manager's backside booted.

One thing you can't blame the manager for is the film. He's landed with the programme whether he likes it or not.

You don't have to be, and if you feel strongly enough about it you should write to the Director of Programme Booking at head office.

WARD'S LAW: Join a cinema queue and see the army.

COMPENSATION

Complaining is an expensive and time-consuming business. There are the telephone calls, the wasted journeys to return faulty goods, the expense and irritation of writing letters just to point out other people's mistakes, the unnecessary wear and tear on your nerves and shoe leather.

Since none of this was your doing, it seems unreasonable to expect you to be inconvenienced *and* put out of pocket.

How do you get the enemy to pay up?

1. 'Fine' firms every time they make a mistake that involves you in unnecessary work. Deduct 10p from your phone bill or bank charges for every letter you have to write pointing out that they boobed.

2. Ask to be reimbursed for your 'expenses'. When you make a long or expensive journey to return faulty goods, for instance, you should point this out to the shopkeeper and ask for an appropriate deduction or refund. He'll almost certainly tell you where to get off, but at least you've let him know that he's dealing with one of the awkward squad.

If you haven't yet paid, or if you have an account, you can deduct your expenses from your next bill, of course, though you must be sure to write to the firm explaining your reasons for doing so.

3. Refuse to be inconvenienced when something you have bought goes wrong. Say you have bought a new car or an electric fire that packs up. Having parted with your money,

why should you now have to walk or freeze to death? Insist that either they supply you with a new car or lend you free of charge a replacement while yours is being repaired. Under the Supply of Goods (Implied Terms) Act, this is your *right*.

WARD'S LAW: Only a fool or a rich man pays for other people's mistakes.

COMPLAINTS
DEPARTMENTS

Complaints departments are the new boom industry of our time. Some of them, it seems, are almost as big as the organizations they serve and protect so loyally. They're not very often called complaints departments these days, but don't be fooled by that. Complaints are euphemistically

referred to as *representations* and the staff who have to sort out the cock-ups are grandly called *conciliators*. It all adds up to the same thing, though: a complaints department. Complaints departments are, by their very existence, an admission of a company's incompetence and failure. They say, in effect, *We have so many dissatisfied customers that we have to have a whole department to deal with them. Please take your place in the queue.*

Unfortunately, complaints departments – also called 'customer relations' – are no more efficient than the shoe department or the household furnishing department that keeps them so busy.

Manned by professional fobbers-off who have grown accustomed to the appalling misfortunes that befall their customers, complaints departments rarely have either the interest or the authority to deal with your problems as you would wish. But they are a blessing to those they protect because their expert apologists get you off the backs of the idle and the incompetent who let you down.

Since you didn't do business with the complaints department in the first place, you should let it be known that their excuses are acceptable only when accompanied by a cheque.

WARD'S LAW: Don't take 'sorry' for an answer.

COMPUTERS

Very occasionally, once in a while, every now and then, a computer makes a mistake.

There was the little old lady aged 93 who received a letter from the education authorities summoning her to court for non-attendance at school.

There was the computer that discharged an airman from the RAF because he was pregnant.

Then there was the Barclays Bank computer that very kindly paid £29,000 of someone else's money into my account.

Well, none of us is perfect.

The trouble is, computers are even less ready to admit they've made a mistake than bank clerks. If a computer decides you're dead, you're more dead than if you were twelve feet under the sod.

How do you tell a computer it has boobed?

All computers have human assistants called 'data processing managers'. If you feel you have become a victim of computer error, write to the firm's Data Processing Manager asking him politely if he wouldn't mind having a quiet word with his infernal machine. Send a copy to the Managing Director.

If that doesn't work, then you will have to take steps to confuse the computer in the hope of inducing a nervous breakdown.

How do you do this?

Simple. If you get a bill for £2.50, overpay by sending off a cheque for £2.52.

Spell your name differently each time. If the computer has come to know you as Roy G. Smith, sign your name G. Roy Smith, or even George Smith. Send it a cheque without signing it.

If that doesn't bring it to heel, try hitting it where it hurts most – straight between its magnetic 'eyes'.

Brush the back of the coded numbers on your cheques with metallic ink, or cut out one of the numbers with a razor blade. Cut any computer punch cards the machine sends you into three or four strips, then Sellotape them together so that the slightly misshapen whole will never again fit into a ledger.

This way you can always be assured of the personal touch in all your dealings with computers.

NEVER IGNORE A COMPUTER. Computers are hungry animals, and need a constant diet of cheques and paperwork to keep them happy.

HUMOUR A COMPUTER. If it's generous enough to send you a bill for £0.000000, at least have the courtesy to send it back a cheque for £0.000000.

If it is under the impression that your name is Arthur Hedgerow and keeps sending *you* cheques every month, don't insult it by pointing out its mistake. Change your name to Arthur Hedgerow by deed poll and write back thanking it.

WARD'S LAW: Computers are only human.

CORPORATIONS

Business corporations are like dinosaurs: large, slow-moving, thick-skinned – and however hard you tread on their tails, nothing ever gets through to the head.

At the head of most corporations is a man who hasn't the foggiest what's going on in his own company outside the boardroom and the Stock Exchange Index. It's hardly surprising because under him, from his secretary and deputy downwards, are hundreds, maybe thousands, of employees who are united by one common cause: *to keep the truth from him.*

Whenever I meet the Chairman of a big organization, I reel off every unhappy experience I've had with his product or company, reasoning that in the office he's told only what he wants to hear. Most are appalled when they hear what's going on.

The Chairman would be equally horrified to hear that you've already had three motors in your washing machine and have been waiting five months for the fourth to be fitted. The problem is getting through to him. He's undoubtedly surrounded by over-protective secretaries and personal assistants who don't want him to be bothered with trifles – or anything that's going to land one of them right in it.

Before you can get through to the head of a large company, you have to know his name. Ring the firm and ask to speak to the managing director's secretary. Tell her you wish to write to the Chairman personally about the wonderful attention and co-operation you have received from the firm and could you please have his name and correct business address.

If you receive an unsatisfactory reply to your letter from someone who is clearly a long way down from the Chairman write to the Chairman again, this time marking the envelope Private and Confidential.

Apologize for this deception but say that you felt sure he never saw your original letter or he would have acted on it. That should do the trick. Failing that, write to him at his home address.

If he's not in the telephone book, he might be in *Who's Who*, or the *Directory of Directors*, both of which you will find in your local library and should give his address. The *Stock Exchange Year Book* is also a useful source of information about the executives of Limited Companies.

Taking on a corporation is very much a David-*v*-Goliath situation: you can bring them down, but you have to know exactly where to aim.

The weak spot of every organization is its reputation. (See 'Publicity'.) It has probably taken years and millions of pounds' worth of advertising to build it up, and it is intensely irritating for managing directors and the like to see the

WE ARE NO FLY BY NIGHT
ORGANISATION

goodwill rapidly being eroded by a nobody with a problem.

(*A Mr George Lough-Atkins of Southminster, Essex, caused the mighty Hoover organization considerable embarrassment by burying his faulty Hoover Keymatic washing machine at sea. Pictures of the 'burial' in the papers next day occupied about £100,000 worth of advertising space.*)

If you keep chipping away at the stonework for long enough, someone up there is going to say, 'For Christ's sake shut that bloody man up, will you?'

And you will get what you want.

WARD'S LAW: David slew Goliath with a letter to the newspapers.

COUNTER-THUMPING

As a substitute for wife-beating, kicking the car, mugging an old lady or throwing up your job, thumping a counter is a harmless safety-valve with considerable therapeutic value.

But as a battle tactic, it's about as successful as a hara-kiri pilot who misses his target.

You make a personal enemy of your opponent. You show yourself to be unreasonable, uncontrollable. And – whatever it was that provoked your wrath – your abuse puts the other side firmly in the right.

WARD'S LAW: The successful complainer is a reasonable complainer.

DEMOS

Demos have been an effective form of protest in this country ever since Wat Tyler led the peasants' revolt in 1381*. Governments have been toppled, laws changed, motorways diverted, airports re-sited.

How?

First of all, they cause officialdom a great deal of embarrassment by all the publicity they attract. Secondly, they tend to gather more support the longer they are allowed to last.

In a democracy like ours, where politicians depend on votes, and business organizations need customers' goodwill to survive, no one can afford to ignore five thousand, five hundred, fifty, or even five voices of protest raised in unison. As Chairman Mao said, 'All views that underestimate the strength of the people are wrong.' Or, to put it another way: far easier to give in to the demands of the protesters than have 500 sheep blocking the MP's car park at the House of Commons all afternoon.

When all the usual democratic procedures have failed – i.e., when you have asked nicely and been turned down – then you must try more revolutionary tactics.

Organizing a demo calls for a good deal of planning and hard work, but it can also be a lot of fun.

How many demonstrators do you need?

It depends on the size of the enemy, the stakes you are

---

* *For his troubles, Wat Tyler got run through by the Lord Mayor of London. It's something you might bear in mind before you organize a protest march to the Mansion House.*

playing for, how you deploy your forces. Half-a-dozen will be enough if you're campaigning for a zebra crossing near your home. Five thousand might not be enough if you want to stop the Government building London's third airport in Hyde Park.

But obviously, whatever your fight, your strength is in numbers. The more people you can persuade to join your demo, the more successful it will be. One hundred protesters are a hundred times more effective than one.

One-man demos should be avoided if possible, since lone protesters tend to be dismissed as cranks. One man walking stark naked down Whitehall, for instance, is quite likely to be carried off to the funny farm without anyone paying the slightest attention. But if five hundred people stripped off and presented themselves at the door of No. 10, then people would start wondering what cause moved so many people

to take such drastic action. What's more, the police can't possibly arrest five hundred people.

How do you recruit your fighting force?

By stopping people in the street, writing to the local newspaper, putting up posters, lobbying members of your wife's knitting circle . . . by making sure that everyone who might have a vested interest in your battle knows about it. It doesn't take long to raise a Mum's Army.

What sort of demo should you organize?

That depends on whether you are:

1. Planning to dig in for a long-term battle with the invisible bureaucrats who want to run a motorway through your garden. Or
2. Intending to make a one-off protest to make your point.

Let's take the one-off demo first.

As the aim is to get as much TV and press publicity as possible for your cause, you must try to make it as dramatic – and as entertaining – as possible.

Housewives in Bolton, Lancs, had the right idea when they did their weekly wash in the fountains in front of the Town Hall. They were protesting about a decision to close the town's wash-houses.

Five hundred villagers from the picturesque hamlet of Wooten Wawn, near Stratford, wanted the Environment Minister, Mr Peter Walker, to know what they thought about a plan to build a huge incinerator near their homes. So they called in at Mr Walker's home one Sunday afternoon to tell him. All five hundred of them.

'How would you feel if five hundred people came to your private house on a Sunday afternoon without being invited?' the hurt Mr Walker later asked reporters.

Exactly.

Irish Women's Lib protesters made their point, too,

when they pelted Dublin Customs officers with contraceptives to protest about the absurd ban on contraceptives.

Chaining yourself to the railings of Buckingham Palace or the Houses of Parliament is hardly original, but this old Suffragette ploy never fails to draw a crowd and cause a lot of commotion while a policeman rushes off to find a hacksaw.

But don't forget to let the Press, TV and local radio news desks know about your demo, and to take along placards so that if your picture gets in the news, so will your slogan.

When you're fighting a long-term war against bureaucracy over a planning decision, the actual demo – and there may have to be many of them – is only a part of the overall battle strategy that you must plan.

You have to organize protest meetings to whip up support, get a petition together, form a strategic planning committee to draw up the battle plans, attend planning inquiries, lodge appeals, lobby MPs and local celebrities to back you. You will need to raise a fighting fund so you can employ the best lawyers, architects and scientists to fight the enemy on an equal footing.

It sounds like a formidable task, but the enemy can be beaten and, indeed, is often beaten by public-spirited citizens who refuse to be pushed around by faceless bureaucrats in Whitehall.

The sit-down demo

This is probably the best kind of demo of all, because it involves nothing more strenuous than remaining in your seat.

It is the only known deterrent against those in the public transport business who, having promised to take us from A to B, try to drop us off at $A + \frac{1}{4}$.

One hundred holidaymakers on a Channel Airways Comet jet staged a sit-in demo with great success when they landed at Stansted instead of at Manchester. They refused to budge until another aircraft arrived to take them to their proper destination.

But the sit-in works just as effectively on the less glamorous setting of a train, a bus, or the Tube. Rebels on the Northern Line won a great victory against London Transport when they defied an 'All Change!' cry and demanded that their Tube train continue to the end of the line.

An essential ingredient of the success of the sit-in however is the co-operation of your fellow passengers. Otherwise you might easily find that you spend an extremely cold and lonely night alone in the railway sidings at Cockfosters.

WARD'S LAW: Embarrass and bully the enemy into submission.

DENTISTS

I'm on very good terms with my dentist and he hurts me one hell of a lot. I dread to think what he'd do with that drill if I ever did anything to upset him. Ouch!

So I think the first thing you have to do if you're going to put the boot in is to find yourself another dentist.

Private dentists always welcome new customers, but their National Health Service brethren, overworked and underpaid as they are, hardly go out of their way to seek extra patients. And, unlike doctors, they are not obliged to treat you, however much agony you're in.

How you set about complaining about your dentist depends on whether you are a private or NHS patient.

NHS DENTISTS

NHS dentists are self-employed and work on a piece-work basis under contract to a Family Practitioner Committee, acting as agents for the Department of Health and Social Security. Unlike NHS doctors, dentists do not *have* to give you treatment. It's up to you to find one willing to take you on as an NHS patient. For the money you spend on phone calls trying to find one, you could have your front teeth capped privately.

Having found an NHS dentist, you may be dismayed to discover that he wants to turn you into a private patient and charge you for all but the most routine dental work. This, alas, he is perfectly entitled to do. You, similarly, are perfectly entitled to get up out of the chair and continue your search for a more co-operative NHS dentist.

If (when you eventually find a dentist) he does something dreadful, like extract all the wrong teeth after mixing up your X-rays with another patient's, you can of course sue him. But you should also complain to the Family Practitioner Committee. Write to the Secretary. The address is in the phone book, under F, and you must make your complaint within eight weeks of the treatment you're complaining about.

But you'll find the Family Practitioner Committee isn't so much worried about the state of your teeth as about whether or not your dentist is guilty of a breach of his contract. If it decides he is, he might be reprimanded. On the other hand, he might have the Committee's fullest sympathy for having such a difficult patient as you.

The Committee also ought to be informed if you feel your dentist's conduct is less than 'professional'. For instance,

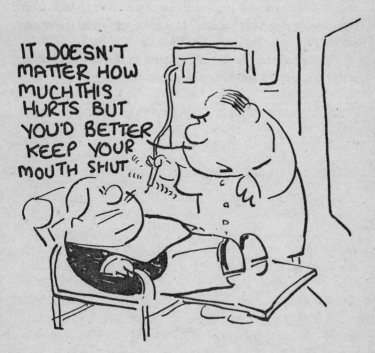

dentists must not breathe whisky fumes over their patients. They must do the job conscientiously and to the best of their ability. Their surgery should be clean, hygienic and orderly.

In serious cases the complaint would be forwarded to the Secretary of State for Health and Social Services, with a recommendation to dock his pay or even expel him from practising in the NHS. But, as the Health Service is so short of dentists, this is fairly unlikely.

If your complaint is dismissed you can appeal to the Secretary of State. Good luck! You'll need it.

There is also a body called the General Dental Council which is the dental equivalent of the General Medical Council, though no less stuffy, alas. All dentists have to be registered with the Council and can be struck off for 'infamous or disgraceful conduct'.

This could be anything from making love to an anaesthetized lady patient (or, for that matter, making love to an *un*anaesthetized lady patient) to riding a bicycle the wrong way down a one-way street in the nude.

Address your bizarre allegations to the Registrar who, if he takes them seriously enough, will ask you to make a formal statement. Your dentist might end up before a disciplinary committee and, after a public hearing, be struck off.

PRIVATE DENTISTS

They get off a bit lighter than their NHS colleagues because they only have to answer to the General Dental Council who aren't interested in complaints about bad treatment or disputes about fees. The Council is however supposed to maintain high standards in the profession and, even if you weren't raped in the dentist's chair, you are entitled to register a formal complaint about unprofessional conduct. It could lead to a ticking-off, but if twenty other patients have all said the same thing, the dentist could really be in trouble.

Can you SUE a dentist?

Yes, why not? If you have spent £100 or more on false teeth that hurt you so much you can never wear them, then you can sue for your money back in the County Court under the small claims procedure. (See Suing.)

WARD'S LAW: A tooth for a tooth, and a tooth for a tooth.

DOCTORS

Doctor Ward will now prescribe short courses of treatment for some common ills afflicting doctors' patients on the ailing National Health.

QUESTION: My doctor doesn't care. Who does?

ANSWER: Your local Community Health Council, which represents patients' views in disputes with the Health Service and helps fight patients' battles. You'll find the address in the telephone book.

QUESTION: I don't have any confidence in my GP. He never examines me thoroughly, he's generally unsympathetic and he seems to be more interested in his golf bag than my health.

ANSWER: I would diagnose this as a terminal case. Find another doctor. If you don't know one, your local Family Practitioner Committee has a list of all the doctors in your area. The Committee's address is in the telephone book under Health Service.

You don't have to tell your old doctor that you wish to change, either, which will spare you a lot of embarrassment. Just send your medical card to the Family Practitioner Committee with a letter saying you want a transfer from Dr A to Dr B. Before you sack your old doctor, however, it's not a bad idea to have a new one lined up. You don't have to give a reason for switching doctors, incidentally.

QUESTION: I can't get a doctor to take me on at all. I've telephoned twenty-three and they all say they're too busy to take on any new patients. What can I do?

ANSWER: Many doctors are already stretched almost

to breaking point and they are not compelled to have you as a permanent patient. If you are ill, however, a National Health doctor is obliged to treat you until you can get fixed up elsewhere. If you still can't find a doctor, write to the Family Practitioner Committee – and it's then up to the Committee to find a doctor.

QUESTION: What happens if someone is desperately ill – during the night, for instance – and your doctor refuses to turn out?

ANSWER: Doctors aren't automatically obliged to turn out but if they have reason to suppose the patient is critically ill, it could be considered to be 'serious professional misconduct' not to do so. A complaint to the Administrator of Family Practitioner Services at the Area Health Authority could lead to a reprimand, to his pay being docked, or – in serious cases – to his being struck off the Medical Register.

But that doesn't solve the problem of getting a doctor round at the moment when you need one. Be as persuasive as possible and, if that doesn't work, become as doggedly persistent as you can without the conversation degenerating into a shouting match. Call back again, repeating the seriousness of the situation and making it clear that you will hold him (or her) responsible for the consequences. If that doesn't work either, then you have no alternative but to dial 999 for an ambulance, or to take the patient yourself to the casualty department of the nearest hospital.

Disputes of this sort are nearly always won by doctors, who claim afterwards that they weren't told fully what the patient's symptoms were. To protect yourself – and with a view to nailing the guilty doctor later – write down a list of the symptoms and make sure the telephone conversation with the reluctant medic is witnessed by a friend. Victory may then be yours – too late to bring back a loved one, perhaps, but perhaps in time to save others.

QUESTION: My doctor's practice is a disgrace. The surgery is dirty, badly run and the bossy over-protective receptionist sometimes makes you wait days to see the doctor. Is there a known cure?

ANSWER: When you see your doctor, you should make sure that he is aware you've been waiting for days to see him. If the receptionist is that bossy, he might not know. But if the whole place is a shambles, the chances are he knows and doesn't care. Seek the help and advice of your local Community Health Council.

QUESTION: My doctor seems to take my illness rather lightly. I've asked for a second opinion, or to see a specialist, but he refuses, saying it's not necessary. Can I insist?

ANSWER: Pile on the agony a bit and, if he still doesn't give way, either change your GP or pay to see a private GP and ask him to refer you to a specialist under the National Health. If there's nothing wrong with you, then at least you now have peace of mind. If there *was* something wrong with you, you're well rid of the GP who dragged his heels.

QUESTION: Can a patient sue for negligence or for a wrong diagnosis?

ANSWER: Doctors must exercise 'reasonable skill' and 'reasonable care' when they are treating patients – whether on the National Health or privately – and if they don't, then you can sue them for negligence. The problem here is getting the evidence, since doctors aren't inclined to rat on each other.

If you have difficulty in finding a doctor who will give you an independent examination and stand up in court on your behalf, the British Academy of Forensic Sciences will supply the name of a medical expert who will help you.

But first of all you need a solicitor – a special sort of solicitor, not the one who helped you buy your house. You need a lawyer with experience in the field of medical negligence. Your Community Health Council should know of one. If not, contact the Patients Association.

QUESTION: What are the chances of success in complaining about doctors?

ANSWER: The prognosis is not very encouraging, I'm afraid, on account of the fact that the medical profession looks after itself with all the dedicated self-interest of the Mafia. For instance, there's a Catch-22-type condition which says that you must make your complaint to the Family Practitioner Committee within eight weeks of the incident you're complaining about. However, it could be six months before you discover that you have three broken ribs and not the indigestion your doctor has been treating you for. Result: complaint dismissed because it's more than eight weeks since he started prescribing Rennies for your broken ribs.

Don't bother complaining about the doc's disagreeable bedside manner, by the way; good manners are outside the doctor's terms of service.

QUESTION: Any chance of getting my doctor struck off?

ANSWER: Not much, no. The General Medical Council, to which every doctor in Britain must belong in order to practise, has the power to strike off any doctor whom it finds guilty of 'serious professional misconduct'. Just what constitutes 'serious professional misconduct' they don't say, but it has to be pretty serious. Usually it involves being caught *in flagrante delicto* with a patient.

If you feel 'serious professional misconduct' aptly describes your doctor's behaviour or treatment, then you should write to the Registrar of the GMC saying you wish to make a formal complaint. If he decides it is a matter for the Council, you will have to make a sworn statement.

PRIVATE DOCTORS

Private doctors, as their name implies, don't have to answer to the health authorities. They answer only to themselves, God, the courts and the GMC. Unless you actually believe your private doctor is a public menace, far easier – since you are paying him for his services – to find yourself another doctor.

CONSULTANTS

Private consultants treating a patient in an NHS hospital are doing so only by permission of the Area Health Authority. (See 'Hospitals'.) If you are not satisfied with the treatment you have been receiving, you should make your feelings forcefully known to the Area Health Authority, who may withdraw their public-funded facilities.

WARD'S LAW: Ailing doctors need to be seen to.

EMPLOYERS

If you are fired unfairly, or your life at work is made so intolerable that you are forced to resign, you may feel inclined to haul your boss in front of an Industrial Tribunal. You and your former employer can then fight it out in front of a three-strong panel of arbitrators who will decide whether or not you have been unjustly dismissed and how much compensation you should receive.

Most cases are settled before they even get to court, but those that do seem to indicate you have a good chance of winning – or at least losing your job with more than just your card.

Mohammed Ayub, a Vauxhall car production worker sacked for sleeping on the job, was awarded £903 compensation; Richard Elvidge, a trainee chef at Claridge's, who was fired for 'culinary disasters', collected £1,050 from his ex-employers.

Industrial tribunals protect employees' rights in all sorts of situation. (See Sex discrimination and Race discrimination.) Among other things, they fix fair redundancy payments and will, for instance, order an employer to keep a pregnant woman's job open so that she can return to it after she has had her baby. They will even order a boss to reinstate a sacked worker. Alan Turner, sent packing with his cello from the Northern Sinfonia Orchestra for 'poor playing and bad behaviour', was reinstated by order of a tribunal.

How do you arraign your employers before a tribunal? Go to any Job Centre or employment office and ask for form IT 1. Fill it in and send it off to the Central Office of

Industrial Tribunals, who will send it on to a regional office and inform ACAS, the Advisory, Conciliation and Arbitration Service. A 'conciliator' will get in touch and offer to reach a settlement acceptable to both sides.

If you want, you can skip the form-filling to begin with and get in touch directly with ACAS who, in confidence, will let you know just how strong they think your case is. They will also negotiate as a go-between with your boss. But if the case does go to a tribunal, form IT 1 has to be filled in.

The tribunal consists of a chairman who is a lawyer and two others – one a union nominee and the other an employers' representative. As the atmosphere is informal, you're not supposed to need a lawyer – but I'm not certain I'd want to go it alone against a couple of barristers putting the boss's case. You can't claim legal expenses against the other side, but your union might be willing to foot the bill for you.

The tribunal's decision may be made known at the hearing, or the court may announce its decision later. In any event, if you lose you can appeal to the Employment Appeal Tribunal.

WARD'S LAW: Go to the Industrial Tribunal fired with determination.

ESCALATING A
COMPLAINT

(or: how to take it to the top)

Cock-ups are often the result of a simple human or mechanical error. A clerk forgets to make a note in the order book. A secretary takes a week's sick leave to go on holiday with her boy friend, leaving a memo about your lawnmower in her Kleenex drawer.

A pleasant telephone call or letter to the right man (A) will often sort out the problem in minutes. No need for threats, angry letters, telegrams to the managing director.

If that doesn't produce results, however, you have to escalate the complaint.

Write to A's immediate boss (B) asking him to sort out your problem. Mention A's incompetence, by all means, but don't let it become more important than your original object – getting your lawnmower back – or you'll get a letter back apologizing for A's sloth, but making no mention of your mower.

If you still don't get anywhere then you have no alternative but to take it to the top.

The bloke who employs all these cretins might hold the title of Managing Director, General Manager, President or Chairman. Find his name and title from someone on the switchboard and also his business address if there is a head office.

When you write or phone, be scrupulously polite and reasonable. He will already be looking for someone to blame, and if you come over as yet another aggressive, difficult and unreasonable customer, his sympathies will be with his incompetent staff and not you.

Sometimes, of course, it pays to go straight to the top without wasting time arguing and pleading with underdogs.

When newsagent Alan Skelton, of Ridgeway, near Chesterfield, learned that he would be getting no Sunday lunch because of a power failure, he telephoned the then Energy Secretary Eric Varley who lived near by.

Surprise, surprise, the lights soon came on and Mr Skelton had his Sunday roast.

WARD'S LAW: There's always someone above the person you're complaining to.

ETIQUETTE

Great complainers, like great soldiers, aren't judged only on results. It is also important to observe certain social niceties and to do it with style and dignity.

For instance, never allow yourself to get involved in a row in front of your wife or girl-friend (or husband, or boy-friend). It's embarrassing for your partner and, since the enemy will suspect you of showing off, it also puts you at a moral disadvantage.

This is not to say that you should abrogate your rights to complain every time you go on a date – although a lot of restaurateurs bank on that.

When you have a complaint or a query over the bill, ask discreetly to speak to the manager and quietly tell him your problem. If he is unhelpful, tell him you are not satisfied and will pursue the matter tomorrow with his superiors.

WARD'S LAW: Don't be embarrassed into submission.

EVIDENCE

Let me tell you a true story with a moral and a happy ending. A few years ago I was walking home from the office when my gaze was drawn to an extremely pretty girl on the other side of the road.

So taken with her was I that I failed to notice that a large manhole cover had been removed from the pavement – and I plunged ten feet down an abyss, landing on top of an Irish navvy and knocking my front teeth out.

No, I didn't marry the girl. I sued the cable-laying company who hadn't put a barrier round the hole.

When my solicitor wrote to the cable-layers, they denied all knowledge of the accident. They even denied that they had ever laid cables on that particular street. They added that they were indeed sorry to hear of my unexpected descent, and suggested that perhaps next time I would look where I was going.

The happy ending is that I sued them and they settled £500 out of court.

And the moral is this: I was able to prove my case only because, bruised and broken though I was, I sat up on the pavement and wrote down the names of the cable company, the Irish navvy I fell on, his mates, the foreman and a couple of passers-by who saw me disappear into the bowels of the earth.

I HAD EVIDENCE.

It's not enough these days to be in the right – you've got to be able to prove it. And if you can't, you might as well be in the wrong.

PERHAPS THIS WILL REFRESH YOUR MEMORY...

What 'evidence' do you need?

Well, names for a start. Always try to have the name (or number) of the person you're complaining about. There's no point complaining about 'a policeman in blue with a funny hat on'. There are more than 100,000 of them in Britain.

Awkward cusses refuse to give their name in an argument, of course, but there are other ways of establishing identity. I once took a photograph of a particularly rude bus conductor who refused to give me his name, and pinned it to my letter of complaint. For a moment I thought he was going to attack me with his ticket machine. If you don't have a camera handy, note a good description of the person, plus the registration number of his bus or whatever.

Dates and times can be vital to establishing your claim, too. A temporary 'disaster diary' noting abortive telephone calls and visits by servicemen makes the enemy look extremely foolish and is riveting reading if you want to bring the Press in on your side at any time.

Do a Nixon and tape-record important telephone

conversations, even. Send important letters by Recorded Delivery so that the enemy can't claim they never received them.

You must also be prepared to gather scientific evidence to support your arguments. There are laboratories all over Britain who are prepared to test everything from clothes, to food, to electrical goods *and* provide you with a well-documented report that can be produced as evidence in court.

Where are these testing laboratories and how much do they charge?

If it's evidence about food that you want, then you might be able to persuade the Health Officer at the Town Hall to get it tested for you free of charge. Failing that, get in touch with the Royal Institute of Chemistry and ask for the address of the nearest public analyst.

The Retail Trading Standards Association has a list of laboratories that can test a wide variety of other goods – not to mention a laboratory of its own, where scientists spend their lives dismantling washing machines and examining shrunken non-shrinkables through microscopes. Write to the Association for advice. The British Standards Institute also has a testing centre. If they can't help, they'll almost certainly be able to put you in touch with a bunch of boffins who can.

One last word of advice that is so often forgotten: ALWAYS keep a carbon copy of any letter you write, along with all the letters you receive.

WARD'S LAW: Evidence is ammunition for your guns.

EXCUSES

Have you noticed how nearly all service vans mysteriously break down on their way to your home? The funny thing is, you never actually *see* a service van that has broken down.

It's just another example of the ill-luck that seems to dog any firm you deal with. Flu wipes out whole departments in mid-July, vital spare parts are marooned by strikes, good weather creates an unexpected shortage of supplies, bad weather delays deliveries.

The enemy is full of excuses, just as old barns are full of bats.

The fall-guy of every big organization these days is the computer. People blame computers like they used to blame the war. 'Now that it's in the computer, there's nothing we can do,' they say.

Never show any interest or sympathy for the enemy's excuses. Never let them think for one minute that you even believe them.

DISMISS an excuse while they're still blustering their way through it, and say understandingly, 'If you wanted more time, why didn't you say so in the first place?' – and get back to the business of pinning them to when they *are* going to come up with the goods.

CONFUSE the enemy with their own excuses. When they start breaking your heart about a strike at the parent company, say with ill-feigned astonishment, 'But yesterday when I spoke to you, you said it was because you were still waiting for the spare parts to arrive from France.'

Most firms make so many excuses that they can't remember who they fobbed off with the computer excuse and who's been placated with 'the situation' in the Middle East.

WARD'S LAW: Don't let other people's problems become *your* problems.

GAS AND
ELECTRICITY BOARDS

GAS BOARDS

The Gas Board has become something of a national joke.
I say, I say, I say. Have you heard the one about the Gas
Board engineer who . . .?

Not only have we heard it, we've all seen it enacted on
our doorsteps by comedians with tool-bags.

I don't have a magic solution that will bring fitters
round to your home with the correct spare part. I can't stop
the accounts department threatening to cut off your supply
for non-payment of a bill you paid a month ago.

If I could do either of these things I'd be Chairman of
the British Gas Corporation. I can, however, suggest a few
effective counter-measures you can launch when things go
wrong.

But first, a few words of explanation about the power
structure of the gas business.

Britain's gas industry is planned and run on a national
scale by the British Gas Corporation. The head gasman, the
Chairman, is Sir Denis Rooke. The buck stops here.

Under Sir Denis's supreme command, Britain is
divided into twelve gas Regions, formerly known as Gas
Boards. They also have Chairmen, who report directly to
Sir Denis.

The Chairman of each Region has a Service Director,
a Marketing Director, and an Engineering Director. One sells

appliances. The second puts them right when they go wrong. The third makes sure there is gas in the pipes. Under these three are various Area Managers and District Managers in charge of day-to-day chaos. They sound important, but they're not, really.

The most common complaint against all Gas Boards – sorry, Regions – is that their service departments are hopelessly inefficient. Customers can't even get through on the phone to report breakdowns. Engineers don't turn up when they say they will. Or they bring the wrong spare parts with them. Or they promise to come back next day and are never seen again . . .

I'm sure you don't need me to tell you what happens.

But when you see how the service system operates, it's easy to see how mistakes occur. When you ring up the service telephone number, what happens is this:

A girl, who has probably never seen a gas cooker in her life, takes a note of your call. The paper is put on a conveyor belt which takes it to a progress clerk who files a copy of it. From there it passes, with a bit of luck, to a work allocator who decides who will do what jobs and when. A supervisor then issues the final orders.

It only needs someone along the line to sneeze and your job card gets blown into the waste-paper basket.

One solution to your service problem is to put your faith in the system working properly some time and ringing up again and again until one day you strike it lucky.

If you don't have the patience of Job, however, there are other alternatives.

You can do what housewife Jackie Moloney did. After five unsuccessful attempts to get her fridge repaired, she locked a gas fitter in her kitchen and refused to release him until the job was done.

But there are more conventional ways. You can ring:

1. THE SERVICE DIRECTOR. He's at the Region's head office and you'll find the address in the telephone

A VERY FUNNY THING HAPPENED TO ME ON MY WAY FROM OUR HIGH STREET BRANCH...

SPIN! SPIN!

GAS BOARD

directory. Ring up and try to find out his name first, because letters and telephone calls directed at names rather than titles stands a better chance of getting through to their targets.

2. THE PRESS OFFICER. Tell him you were going to tell your local newspaper about the service department's crass inefficiency but you thought it only fair to avoid unpleasantness by giving him a chance to put things right first. It's not his job, so be charming rather than pushy.

3. THE CHAIRMAN. Something should happen when you write to him, but add two days at least while internal memos fly.

4. THE GAS CONSUMER COUNCIL. This is an independent watchdog body that will intercede on your behalf in any dispute with the Gas Board. It's a bit slow, but it does no harm to send them copies of your letters to other departments, just so they know what's going on. Their

address is on the back of your gas bill and also ought to be on display in your local gas showroom.

5. MR ROBIN W. HILL. He's the Service Director of the British Gas Corporation in London and therefore cracks a whip over all the service departments in the country. He's a no-nonsense Scotsman who will put things right when they go wrong. But don't bother him with trivialities: he's got a lot on his plate.

6. THE HOME SERVICE ADVISER. If your cakes don't rise for reasons of a technical rather than a culinary nature, then the Home Service Adviser (normally a woman) will call round to find out why. She is also responsible for the welfare of disabled or elderly consumers.

What should you do when the Board threatens to cut off your supply for non-payment of an account – which you have already settled?

The short answer to this is to send a letter by Recorded Delivery to the regional Chairman stating the facts briefly and warning him that if your gas supply is cut off you will remove yourself and your entire family to a hotel until it is restored and sue him for breach of contract.

If, in the meantime, the men call to cut you off, you do not have to admit them unless they have a court order.

The gas companies have an obligation in law to supply you with gas providing you live within 25 yards of a gas main, and providing you pay your bill, of course. If they cut you off without giving you seven days' notice of disconnection of supply, or when you have already settled your account, they are guilty of an offence under Paragraph 6 of Schedule 4 of the Gas Act, 1972, and are liable to a maximum fine of £20.

If this should happen, all you have to do is pay a visit to your local magistrates' court, ask to see the clerk of the court and say you wish to take out a summons. It is not difficult, and, anyway, the clerk will guide you through the legal jungle. It is also good training if you should later decide to sue the gas company for breach of contract in the County Court.

What should you do if the board threatens to cut off the supply when you HAVEN'T paid the bill?

Well, you could always try paying it. But if you can't, then there's a Code of Practice you ought to know about to prevent unnecessary suffering or hardship by you and your family. The code lays down the circumstances in which Gas and Electricity Boards will or won't disconnect your supply.

They won't cut you off:

IF you agree to make regular payments to pay off the debt.

IF cutting off the supply would cause hardship to young children or old people.

IF there is genuine financial hardship.

However, Gas Board accounts clerks aren't psychic and need to be told these things. Give them plenty of advance notice that you won't be able to pay the bill, and involve the local Social Security office and the council's social services department, who may even help you with the payments. You can't expect to be the only person in Britain with free gas or electricity, so you're only buying time.

ELECTRICITY BOARDS

Electricity Boards don't talk about 'complaints'. They call them 'representations'. They have an awful lot of representations, do Electricity Boards. This is where you should take yours:

To the Area Manager in overall charge of your district. You can find him at the head office of your local Board – the address and telephone number should be on your bill somewhere. Send a copy of any correspondence to the Chairman of the Consultative Council just to show everyone you mean business.

Many of the Electricity Boards also have Customer Service Managers, though the actual title might vary in different parts of the country. Give them the benefit of the doubt by asking them to sort things out, but don't waste too much time with them if they don't seem to be getting on with it. It often turns out to be a fobbing-off job.

But there are always the Consultative Councils who represent the interests of the consumer, and they will weigh in on your side if you're not in any great hurry. They should know about any disputes you have with the Board, if only so that they can try to stop it happening to someone else.

You can find out where your local Consultative Council is from the back of your electricity bill or from your electricity showroom. A quick way to get wheels moving is to contact one of the lay members of the Council – their names and addresses are available (if not on display) at the showroom. Contact them, in a friendly way, at home.

Another useful recipient of 'representations' is the recently set up Electricity Consumers' Council. It's a pressure group backed by the Department of Prices and Consumer Protection and it prides itself on fielding complaints – sorry, representations – to the 'right' people at the Electricity Board. Give them a whirl. There's nothing to lose.

Electricity Boards, incidentally, are under the same *legal* obligations to supply you with power as the gas companies. If they have forgotten this, remind them.

WARD'S LAW: No one can win a battle against a bureaucratic organization without knowing the name and the title of the person he is complaining to.

GUARANTEES

Guarantees certainly look very pretty. Some of them even sound quite reassuring. But they don't really mean very much, because the Supply of Goods (Implied Terms) Act, 1973, is the best guarantee of all.

Your rights in law are protected whatever the guarantee says. The guarantee, for instance, may say that the manufacturers will replace any defective parts free of charge, but you will have to pay the labour charges. You don't.

It may say you have to pay for 'postage, packing and transportation' if it has to be returned to the factory. You don't.

Your contract is with the seller, not the manufacturer, and if the seller or the manufacturer try to pull a fast one on you, tell them where to get off.

But fill in and send off the guarantee card, anyway. It may give you extra protection and it can't take away any rights you already have.

WARD'S LAW: The law is your guarantee.

HEAD OFFICE

The one-man band has, alas, played its own funeral march. The shop on the corner has become just another link in a long chain of stores. The small business with the personal touch has been taken over by the big business with the impersonal touch.

The result is that the bloke in charge can no longer be found 'in the office at the top of the stairs' or 'round the back in the store room'. He's probably a couple of hundred miles away in some concrete monolith known as Head Office. He may not have even heard of the place, still less visited it.

Nevertheless Head Office is where all the important decisions are taken. From here all backsides are kicked, all refunds authorized. Here you will find the ringmaster who

cracks the whip, who holds the hoop while those in the outback jump through it.

When you are losing a battle at a local level, shift your fight to Head Office. All head offices pride themselves on the fact that their branches and subsidiaries look after themselves, leaving them to look after the profits. The aggravation of having to dirty their hands dealing with you should prompt them to find a speedy solution to your problem.

Similarly, no one in a branch office likes head office men sniffing around. Heaven knows what they might uncover. They, too, will want to get you off their back.

Make sure it *is* the head office you get in touch with and not just a local HQ. If the firm itself won't volunteer this information you can look it up yourself in your local library in *Kelly's Manufacturers and Merchants Directory.*

WARD'S LAW: Aim high to hit low.

HE'S IN A MEETING

If executives really were 'in a meeting' as often as their secretaries say they are, there wouldn't be any need for office blocks – just meeting-halls.

The 'meeting' has now become the managerial equivalent of the standard shop-floor excuse, 'The van's broken down.' It's a bit classier, but no more believable.

When a secretary tells you 'He's in a meeting', she can mean any number of things. Such as, 'He came back drunk from lunch and is asleep on the floor in his office.' Or, 'He didn't come back from lunch.' Or, 'It's his day off but his wife doesn't know.'

But more often than not he's in a meeting because he doesn't want to talk to you.

If he can lie to avoid you, then you are entitled to use a little cunning to get him out of that 'meeting'. This one never fails to bring someone to the phone.

'*Is that Mr Brown's office?*'

'*Yes, this is his secretary speaking.*'

'*Mr G. Brown, is that?*'

'*Yes.*'

'*This is the Premium Bond headquarters at Lytham St Annes here, winners' tracing section. Could I speak to Mr Brown* personally *please?*'

It's an offence to impersonate a police officer, but there's nothing to stop you telling his prissy secretary, 'It's his bank, it's rather urgent, I'm afraid.' Or saying, 'My name's

Richardson. Do you know if he's heard about his car yet . . .
he hasn't? Oh dear, well, if I could speak to him . . .'

You can always tell when someone really is at a meeting,
by the way. They call you back as soon as the meeting is
over.

**WARD'S LAW: Meetings end, but excuses go
on for ever.**

HOLIDAYS

I look at it like this: Most of us probably have only twenty or thirty holidays in our lifetimes.

The two or three weeks we are away is the only chance we get all year to escape from our homes and our jobs.

And if the holiday is a disaster, we don't get another crack of the whip for a year.

With these stakes I consider my holiday to be a desperately serious business and I expect others to treat it as such, too.

But all too often, alas, holidays turn out to be, well, no holiday.

Holidaymakers – if you can call us that – find ourselves experiencing ordeals more normally suffered by prisoners of war or refugees. We wait days at airports for a plane to take us somewhere, anywhere. We are shunted from hotel to hotel, unwanted embarrassments every one of us. We are billeted in conditions that compare unfavourably with Sing-Sing. We are kept awake at night and the food is little above subsistence level.

And who has subjected us to these ordeals? The very people whom we paid to make our holiday enjoyable.

The best advice I can give you will come too late if you're reading this on the beach in Benidorm: *prevention is better than cure.* Before you book a package tour, make sure that the travel agent and tour operators are members of ABTA, the Association of British Travel Agents. This is no guarantee of the holiday of a lifetime, of course, but it stacks the cards in your favour and if the holiday firm goes bust or otherwise lets you down, you won't lose out financially or funancially.

If you are taking a charter flight, make sure the flight operator has an ATOL licence. (ATOL stands for Air Travel Organizer's Licence, which is issued by the Civil Aviation Authority only after careful vetting of the operator.) If an ATOL holder goes bust while you're abroad, there's a rescue fund which will pay for your return flight.

When holidays do go wrong, it's important to act fast to put things right *immediately*. Apologies and refunds when you get home are all very well, but they come too late to save your holiday.

If you're travelling independently of a tour operator and haven't paid anything in advance, then you're in a strong position if things aren't what they were cracked up to be. You can just move on to greener pastures.

But when you have already parted with your cash – on a package tour or villa holiday, for instance – you obviously can't do that.

The trouble is, a thousand miles or more from home, we all feel particularly isolated and helpless.

The courier or local rep of the travel firm is usually given a lot of discretion to sort trouble out, and you should make your feelings known to him at once. Give the hotel manager a free character reading, too.

If they haven't solved the problems within a day, then you must by-pass them and send a telegram to the Managing Director of the tour operators.

Forgive my pessimism, but it might be a wise precaution to find out his name and address before you leave England. If not, the address of the firm's head office will probably be somewhere on the brochure.

Give the Managing Director twenty-four hours to act on your telegram and then ring him. Yes, I know it's expensive ringing London from Majorca, but with a bit of cunning you can get them to pay. Find out the name of your courier and book a transfer-charge call in his name. They're bound to accept the call if they think it's from him.

If things are fairly awful, then during the course of your telephone conversation with him you should mention, without being too aggressive and threatening about it, that unless something is done, your next telephone call will be to a national newspaper.

Your next step is to do just that – most national newspapers will accept a transfer-charge call whether they know the caller or not, and they might be quite glad to hear your unhappy holiday story. 'Rebel holidaymaker' stories are a veritable godsend for desperate news editors during Fleet Street's 'silly season'.

You should also send a telegram to the Association of British Travel Agents asking them to intercede urgently on your behalf. It needn't be a long cable – just so long as it has your name, the name of the tour operators, and the number of the holiday you booked.

If you still don't get anywhere, you're either very unlucky or very unreasonable.

Following up a complaint when you get home is much

less nerve-racking. It helps if you make an official complaint at the time to the company or the courier.

Write to the Managing Director of the tour operators at head office and send a copy to the Conciliation Department at ABTA, with an accompanying note saying 'For Your Information'.

If you don't get satisfaction from the firm, take it up with ABTA, who have a free conciliation service for sorting out disputes. The next move, if you're still not getting anywhere, is to use ABTA's arbitration scheme. All members have to accept the arbitrator's final decision. Arbitration will cost you £10, plus £5 for each other adult associated with your claim (£2 if they're family), but it's fair, and if you have been hard done by, you should win your case, and get a proportionate refund, plus the £10 dispute deposit back.

What you need to win your case is convincing *evidence*. Keep the glossy brochure that enticed you to embark on the disastrous holiday, noting all the broken promises. Some holiday snaps of the more incriminating evidence might help your case. If the brochure promised you a swimming-pool at your hotel, for instance, take a picture of the uncompleted rubble-filled hole in the ground. If the food forms a part of your complaint, take some colour snaps of a couple of lunches and dinners.

There is another course of attack open to you, which you may also feel inclined to pursue.

If you feel the brochure describing the holiday was not only misleading but made promises that weren't kept, then you might have a case against the firm under the Trade Descriptions Act, providing it can be shown that the firm were 'reckless' in making these promises.

Your chances of having a happy holiday will be considerably increased, however, if you read the small print on the contract before you sign anything.

Nevertheless, I think it's fair at this point to say that,

with package holidays, you do only get what you pay for. A lot of people pay fifty quid for two weeks in Spain and expect to be put up in the Costa Brava equivalent of Claridges.

But most of the blame for spoiled holidays can be laid on those too glossy travel brochures. Nobody in their right mind believes a washing-powder commercial, but for some reason, everyone expects a travel brochure to tell the truth. Travel agents are, after all, in the business of selling holidays and the brochures are no more than enticing advertisements that paint a rosy picture of a fairly ordinary resort. Like secret codes, they will tell you everything you need to know, providing you know how to 'read' the text and 'interpret' the pictures.

As a veteran package tourist I have learned that all the vital information is contained not in what brochures say and show but in what they *don't* say and show. The trick is to know how to continue the sentence and define a picture where the brochure leaves off.

For instance, here is a typical brochure-type description of a non-existent resort, Para Diso, with those vital missing words in italics. It should help you to form a more accurate impression of what you can look forward to on your next holiday:

Para Diso is famous for its horse-shoe bay whose sandy white beaches are practically deserted *at six o'clock in the morning when this picture was taken. But the crowds soon build up and you would be well advised to be down on the beach by 7.30 if you want to be sure of a place.*

There are all kinds of things to do if you get tired of sunbathing. You can hire pedalos or go water-skiing *or you can do what the family just out of the picture is doing, and spend the day cleaning tar off your clothes with a petrol-soaked rag.*

The clear blue sea is full of red mullet, delicious

when grilled over a charcoal spit, *jellyfish and sea urchins – and empty Ambre Solaire bottles, beer cans and ice-cream cups, which are not so delicious when grilled over a charcoal spit.*

Para Diso is a charming little fishing village where fishermen, pursuing their centuries-old occupation, sit cross-legged in the port mending their nets. Fishermen like Manuel in our picture above, *who comes from the Rent-a-Peasant model agency and who also appears in our brochures on Alassio, Ibiza, Majorca, Nice and Mexico City.*

Try not to miss a trip to the exotic Bella Vista beach, which has a marvellous view of the famous Para Diso caves, as you can see from this picture *taken from the window of one of the express trains that roar past the beach every eleven-and-a-half minutes.*

The situation of your hotel is superb, *unlike the situation of your hotel room whose window opens two feet above the extractor fan from the all-night kitchens*, with wonderful views of the bay *and an uninterrupted view of a building site below, where the cement mixers start turning at 5 am every morning.*

If you're a night-owl there are plenty of night clubs where you can dance the night away *and might as well since three of them are situated only a bottle's throw from your bedroom window and you certainly won't get any sleep.*

You will like the happy smiling service you will find in Para Diso *if you tip the waiter a quid every time you order a Coca-Cola. We had to pay this miserable lot five pounds each to smile like this for our picture.*

The prices are reasonable, too. *Two quid for an ice-cream, three for a Pepsi.*

If it's Beautiful People you're looking for, well, just take a look at these two beauties *who were flown over from Paris after our photographer spent three weeks unsuccessfully scouring Para Diso for a girl worth photographing.*

One thing is certain: you will never find a resort where the sky and sea is so blue, the sand so white or the flowers so colourful as Para Diso. *Our photographer made sure of that by taking with him a case full of filters to make suntans browner, skies bluer, seas clearer, sand whiter and flowers brighter.*

We sincerely hope that you will enjoy your holiday *but don't tell us if you don't.*

WARD'S LAW: Make hell while the sun shines.

HOSPITALS

There's nothing like a short spell in hospital for making most people feel really unwell. Woken up at 6.30 am, fed on prison rations, pushed around by bossy nurses, neglected by overworked doctors . . . they certainly thought they were ill when they were admitted, but it isn't until our wonderful hospital service has fed them through the National Health mincer that they realize that, in comparison, they weren't ill at all.

What we need are post-hospital hospitals, to treat patients from the effects of a stay in hospital.

Hospitals are the one exception to all the laws of complaining. Because you are bed-bound, in a strange environment and not feeling your best, you are wholly dependent on those who serve you. Complaining about a hospital when you are still a patient there is quite likely to make matters worse. You might be made to suffer for it. You are almost certainly going to cast yourself in the role of what is known among hospital staffs as The Unpopular Patient.

The Royal College of Nursing, with admirable honesty, conducted a survey into The Unpopular Patient a couple of years ago. It found that unpopular patients – i.e. inmates who for various reasons were not liked by the staff – received considerably worse care and treatment than the popular ones.

'*The nurses seemed to think that ignoring patients was the most powerful deterrent to unacceptable behaviour, and, certainly, some unpopular patients had requests ignored or forgotten,*' says the report.

The report continues: '*The patients whom the nurses*

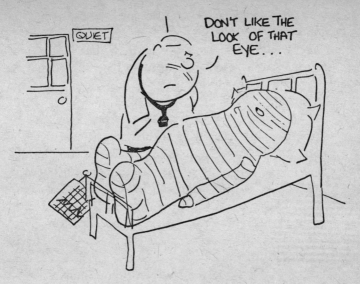

indicated they did not enjoy looking after fell into two main groups. There were those who indicated that they were not happy to be in the ward, or with what was being done for them, by grumbling and complaining or otherwise demanding attention. In the second group were those whom the nurses felt did not need to be in hospital, or should not be in that particular ward, and whose personalities did not outweigh this judgement.'

Get the message? Fortunately the report does give you some idea about how to be one of those patients whom nurses *do* enjoy looking after:

'Patients the nurses enjoyed caring for were able to communicate readily with the nurses, knew the nurses' names, were able to joke and laugh with the nurses, and co-operated in being helped to get well and expressed determination to do so.'

But sometimes even the most popular patient, the most reasonable and patient patient, has very real grounds for complaint.

Day-to-day running of the wards is the responsibility of the ward sister, who usually tours her territory at least once a day. She also has the ear of the doctor and therefore exercises very considerable influence over the treatment and care you receive.

Don't bother her with petty moans, but if a serious mistake has been made, she ought to be told about it, if only so that she can prevent it happening again to some other patient.

If you feel that your complaint is too serious to be confined to ward level, you should take it up with the Hospital Administrator, who is responsible for running the hospital. He is not a doctor, but everything that happens in the hospital is in his charge and he answers to the Area Health Authority, which answers to the Regional Health Authority, which in turn answers to the Department of Health and Social Security. There are ninety Area Health Authorities in Britain.

When you write to the Hospital Administrator, send a copy of your letter to the Secretary of the Community Health Council for that district. The council represents patients' and concerned relatives' views in all disputes. The hospital itself will know the address of the Council, but if you feel too embarrassed to ask, your local Citizens' Advice Bureau will find out for you.

It's worth involving the Community Health Council early in a complaint. They know all the local administrators and consultants and will have heard about similar complaints

to your own. Ask them to write your letter for you, if you feel you need their help.

If the Hospital Administrator is obstructive or unhelpful and your complaint is a serious one, you should go straight to the Ombudsman, wearing his hat as Health Service Commissioner. His address is in the index at the back of this book. He may send one of his officers to interview you about your Health Service disaster story. He has the power to pursue your complaint at the highest level in the Area Health Authority and the Regional Health Authority and if he decides that a terrible wrong has occurred, he will publicly name the guilty men or women in his report to Parliament.

There is also a private organization called the Patients' Association, which has considerable experience of patients' suffering. They, too, will take up your complaint with the appropriate authorities.

But if you have suffered physically or financially because of a clinical mistake made by the hospital or one of the doctors or nurses employed by it, then you need none of these people. What you need is a solicitor experienced in the field of medical negligence. Only a solicitor will be able to win you proper compensation when the surgeon removes your left leg instead of the troublesome wart you came in with.

WARD'S LAW: A smile a day keeps the nurses at bay.

INFLUENCE IN
HIGH PLACES

Let me put it like this: how long do you think Mrs Margaret Thatcher has to wait before the Gas Board fitter calls to adjust her pilot light? Three months? A fortnight? Or the same day that she rang them?

How many restaurants, however crowded, don't have a free table when a gentleman by the name of Snowdon telephones to book a table there?

How many Kissingers find they have been double-booked by an airline and have to wait overnight for the first available flight?

It's amazing how the right name or the right connections never fail to unlock doors that remain firmly shut and bolted to the Smiths, the Joneses (though not the Armstrong-Joneses) and the Wards of this world.

What can we nobodies do with all the wrong friends and no influence?

Well, *you* may know you're a nobody, but *they* don't. Cash in on their creeping, grovelling, toady attitude by letting them think you're someone you're not.

CHANGE YOUR NAME FOR THE DAY. Next time you call a restaurant and a snooty head waiter tells you that they don't have any free tables, ring back half an hour later and say you're Bianca Jagger's private secretary and wish to reserve a table for Mrs Jagger. Suddenly – miraculously even – they will have a table. Not just *a* table. The *best* table.

When you get there, of course, they just as suddenly

GAME, SET
AND MATCH
TO MR. SMOOTHY...

won't have a table any more. Insist that your secretary booked a table by phone and that your surname is Bander-Jagot. The head waiter usually keeps his reservations list by the door, so you may even be able to point to Mrs Jagger's name and explain that he obviously misheard it when taking the booking.

Find out the name of the person the enemy most fears and drop it mercilessly.

A name that works wonders in Trust Houses Forte hotels and restaurants, for instance, is Forte. Sir Charles Forte is the Chairman and any employee with an eye for promotion is going to treat any customer called Forte with a great deal of care and respect – just in case.

Every organization has a magic name that conjures up the VIP treatment that is usually reserved for others.

Say your ten-year-old daughter is in hospital and is not

being looked after as well as you feel she ought to be. A call
to the ward sister from the 'Chairman Train of the Area Health
Authority' inquiring about his niece should assure her of the
very best attention. (The switchboard staff will be able to
tell you the chairman's name.)

Egon Ronay is a name that always improves service in
hotels, I find. An overheard telephone call to him on your
first day will guarantee you a happy stay, and you don't
even have to know him. Book a call to a friend who will be
happy to impersonate the gourmet – and leave the rest to the
indiscretion of the switchboard operator.

Dropping the name of an important organization can be
equally effective. A friend whose bags were lost on a flight
from New York to London rang a senior executive at the
airline when his luggage still hadn't turned up after a week.
He pretended to be a security officer at the Defence Ministry
and urged the airline to step up the search for the bags
because of the 'embarrassment' that certain 'classified
documents' might cause if they fell into the wrong hands.

The suitcases were found in Honolulu that night and
were returned to him the very next day.

**WARD'S LAW: The Royal Train always leaves
on time.**

INSURANCE

The reason why insurance companies so willingly insure your car, your house, your wife, your life, is that they believe that It is never going to happen.

When It does happen, as It so often does, then they are understandably hurt and angry to learn that they have backed yet another loser. They get out the policy and examine the small print to try to find a clause that relieves them of their obligation to pay up.

It's surprising – well, it isn't surprising, actually – how often they find one. I write as one who lost a beach buggy at sea two hours before reading the Marine Disasters exclusion clause in my motor insurance policy.

The one thing you can't insure against is a sharp insurance company wriggling out of its moral obligations, so the best protection of all is to read the policy before it happens, to find out just what you are paying for.

But if this advice comes too late to you, or the insurance company disputes your claim anyway, then there are ways of putting pressure on them.

Don't, whatever you do, fire off an abusive letter to the chairman of a £4,000 million insurance company telling him you'll sue them for every penny they've got unless they replace the £2.50 gold-plated cuff-links you lost on Brighton beach. Insurance companies know their legal rights better than anyone – and yours, too. Baseless legal threats simply make them dig in.

See a solicitor, by all means, and get him to tell you just where you stand, but don't try and go it alone against the big boys. They've got a winning streak a billion pounds long.

Insurance companies will often make 'ex gratia' payments in borderline cases where they believe they are not strictly liable, but where the goodwill is worth more than the sum being claimed.

They won't volunteer this generous gesture. You will have to pressure them into it. Bombard them with letters. If that doesn't work, then start writing to the Chairman at head office. Send a copy of the letter to the British Insurance Association, to which all the main companies belong, asking them to help you sort out the dispute.

When the company realizes you're not going to shut up, they will probably pay up.

INSURANCE BROKERS

A lot of insurance business is done through high-street brokers who will often be able to press a disputed claim against a big company much more effectively than you can. But, equally, you may find yourself having a battle with a villainous broker as well as an insurance company.

There is no official register of brokers – not yet, anyway – but two trade associations try to maintain high standards among their members of the profession – the Insurance Brokers Registration Council, and the British Insurance Brokers Association. If your broker is a member of either of these organizations, you can broaden your battle front and take your fight to them.

WARD'S LAW: Don't let your claim go up in flames, too.

KNOW YOUR RIGHTS

Say nothing, do nothing, before you know where you stand legally.

When you're not in the right, it saves you making a fool of yourself and pursuing lost causes; when you are, it gives you the confidence and determination to press on with the fight.

In the middle of a battle the enemy is hardly going to tell you where to hit them to bring them to their knees, so you must arm yourself with this information beforehand.

Three excellent paperbacks that between them tell you almost everything you need to know are *The Consumer Society and the Law*, by Gordon Borrie and Aubrey L. Diamond (Pelican, £1), *Civil Liberty, the NCCL Guide to your Rights* (Penguin Handbook, £1.75), and *Questions of Law*, by Bill Thomas, the *Jimmy Young Show*'s 'Legal Beagle' (Hamlyn Paperbacks, 95p).

There's also a veritable mine of free information available elsewhere – from your Citizens' Advice Bureau, or from the Office of Fair Trading who produce easy-to-understand leaflets covering most consumer problems.

WARD'S LAW: Fight no battle you are not certain of winning.

LANDLORDS

I expect your landlord wants to put the rent up again. Oh, it's worse than that is it? He wants to put *you* out.

Well, I wouldn't worry too much just yet if I were you. It's probably just a try-on.

Under the Rent Act a private landlord cannot turn you out of your home without a County Court possession order.

Your biggest weapon in any fight against your landlord is to know exactly what your legal position is.

The Citizens' Advice Bureau will tell you what your rights are. If there is a law centre in your neighbourhood you can find out there, too. Then there's Shelter, an organization that helps the homeless and has therefore come across your problem a thousand times before. And possibly there's a housing aid centre near you who know the score, too. All these people will give you free advice about any tenant-landlord problem.

Many landlords, alas, seem strangely unaware of their legal obligations.

They give notice to quit within fourteen days. The minimum period of notice is four weeks *and it must be in writing*.

They charge higher rents than are permitted by law. Check to see whether the flat or house is registered at the nearest Rent Office. You could be paying too much. Even if there is no fixed rent you can ask the Rent Officer to fix a fair rent.

Landlords also commit a number of criminal offences: they fail to issue rent books to weekly tenants; they harass tenants, cutting off their gas, electricity and water to get them out; they evict tenants without first obtaining a court order.

If this sounds remarkably like your landlord then you can make a formal complaint at the Town Clerk's office. Harassment and unlawful eviction carry heavy penalties.

Even if your landlord gets the law on his side and obtains a court order, all is not lost. Ask the court immediately for a twenty-eight-day adjournment and prepare to fight your landlord with the help of the professional advice you have sought.

This is a time when most people turn to their friends for help. If it's comfort and moral support you need, they're the right people. But don't let your friends be your legal advisers, too. They think they know your rights. They probably don't. Leave that to the experts.

LANDLORD COUNCILS

If you are renting your home from the council, you don't have the same protection and security of tenure that a private tenant has.

Although you will have a tenancy agreement with the council, it will set out the strict rules that the tenant must obey – on pain of eviction. Some agreements forbid pets, for instance. But they very rarely mention the council's obligations and responsibilities.

Many tenant associations are now campaigning for fairer tenancy agreements and some councils have even accepted these demands, introducing tenants' charters as legally binding agreements.

The housing-help organizations listed above will help with all your council tenant problems, including repairs disputes. There is another set-up called the National Tenants Organisation which also helps tenants in their battle with official councildom.

WARD'S LAW: Keep your landlord's foot out of your own front door.

LAUNDRIES AND
DRY CLEANERS

It's a thankless life being a launderer or a dry-cleaner. You spend thousands of pounds on the very latest button-crushing and shirt-shredding machine; you manage, with considerable difficulty, to shrink the unshrinkable and make fast colours run; you develop wonderful new chemical processes for converting soft old suede into stiff new cardboard; you return pretty blue-striped sheets to your customers when they only sent you boring white sheets.

But do your customers appreciate all the trouble you have gone to on their behalf? They do not.

Are you one of the many ungrateful customers who make our wonderful dry-cleaners' and launderers' lives a misery? Just as I thought . . .

As you know, what usually happens is this: when you collect your favourite party dress from the cleaners, you can't help noticing that it is a slightly different colour to what it was when you brought it in, and that the seams appear to have come away.

You point this out to the lady behind the counter as she takes your £2.50 for cleaning it, and she says, '*Yes, the manager says they did the best they could, but there's something wrong with the material. He suggests you take it back to the shop you bought it from.*'

At the shop, the buyer looks at your dress in horror. '*They must have boiled it,*' he says. '*We've sold hundreds of these dresses without a single complaint.*'

The dry-cleaner is adamant it's the shop's fault. The shop is adamant it's the dry-cleaner's fault. Now YOU must start to get adamant unless you want to be left with a worthless dress – and pay £2.50 for having it ruined.

Ask them if they are a member of the Association of British Launderers and Cleaners. If they are (and 75 per cent are) say you will refer the matter in writing to the Association's Services Adviser, who will investigate your complaint.

If the Association thinks that a scientific test would settle the dispute, then it will arrange one at an independent laboratory – and it won't cost you anything. And so long as the boffins find in your favour, you will be fairly compensated. Another advantage of dealing with ABLC members is that its launderers and cleaners are obliged to pay you fair compensation if they lose your clothes.

If the Services Adviser's ruling doesn't satisfy you, or the cleaner or launderer isn't a member of ABLC, all is not lost. You can always send the garment to an independent laboratory for testing to find out where the blame lies. (See 'Evidence'.) But, as this costs £10 or more, it's obviously an uneconomic gamble unless the garment is worth a lot of money.

So strike a deal with the dry-cleaners and the shop you bought the dress from. Write to them saying that you will

have the garment tested on the understanding that whoever is to blame pays the testing fee and compensates you for your ruined dress.

But it shouldn't ever come to this. As experts at ruining or losing people's clothes, dry-cleaners and launderers are resigned to the fact that much of their working life is spent writing letters of apology and sending off cheques of compensation.

Some of them are almost too ready to accept the blame, in fact. A friend of mine sent a stinging letter to her laundry when she discovered a bedspread was missing from the box returned to her. Almost by return of post she received a grovelling letter of apology and a cheque.

Two days later she found the bedspread in a cupboard. She had never sent it.

WARD'S LAW: Don't let the laundry take you to the cleaners.

LAWYERS

The trouble with solicitors and barristers is that they are their own judge and jury. File an official complaint against a lawyer and your case will be judged by other lawyers; sue a lawyer and you first have to find a solicitor willing to handle your case. Lawyers, more than anyone, like to be found not guilty of all the charges against them.

Such incestuousness would be intolerable in the Mafia, but with the legal profession, built and sustained by the old-boy network and oversensitive to criticism, it makes it very hard indeed for an outsider with a grievance to put the boot in.

What chance do you have of obtaining justice in your fight against your incompetent legal advisers?

Very little, I am afraid, unless you are particularly determined, or particularly unfortunate in your choice of incompetent lawyers.

SOLICITORS

Solicitors are the most common cause of complaint, not so much for what they do but more for what they don't do. They leave unread letters gathering dust on their shelves, sometimes for years; they don't answer letters; they fail to trace witnesses or to obtain vital scientific information; instead of representing you themselves, they put young or inexperienced clerks in charge of cases; they brief inexperienced barristers; they take inadequate statements; they fraternize with the police or opposing counsel.

If you feel your solicitor has been negligent or incompetent in any way, there are a number of courses of action open to you.

1. You can complain about him to the senior partner of the firm of solicitors he represents, in the hope that a hefty boot up the backside from his boss will make him pull his socks up.

The switchboard girl will tell you the senior partner's name. If you don't like to ask her, or if she is unhelpful, you will find the name in a hefty volume called the *Solicitors Diary and Directory*, a copy of which will be at your local Citizens' Advice Bureau or library. This method doesn't work, of course, if it's the senior partner who is dragging his feet.

2. You can complain to your local Law Society, the address of which you can obtain from a telephone book or the Citizens' Advice Bureau.

Local Law Societies are toothless bulldogs that have no power to strike a solicitor off, and their members tend to live in one another's pockets. But the Secretary might feel bound officially to reprimand your solicitor over a glass of after-dinner port, or at the club-house after a game of golf. So if you feel like stirring things up for your solicitor locally, and no more, the local Law Society is your best bet.

3. You can complain to the Law Society in London, the governing body of the 33,000 members of the legal profession who practise as solicitors (but not barristers).

Briefly, what happens is this: your letter will be read by the Secretary of the Professional Purposes Committee who will either write back and tell you, in polite legalistic terms, to go and get stuffed, or, if he feels there are grounds for enquiring further, will write to the solicitor concerned asking for his side of the story. In which case, he will have to have your permission to send the accused a copy of your letter. This is something to bear in mind while writing it in the first place.

If, after hearing from the solicitor, he feels there has been 'a serious breach of the rules' or 'conduct unbefitting a solicitor', there will be a lot of grunting and groaning and the case will be referred to the Disciplinary Committee.

The Committee can fine a solicitor (though you don't get the money). It can reprimand him. It can even, in very extreme cases, strike him off. It can also, and frequently does, find him not guilty without telling you why.

The Law Society can help you, however, if you feel your solicitor has overcharged you. Write to their Contentious Business Department, giving details of the work done on your behalf, and a copy of the bill. They will look into the matter before the turn of the century.

As soon as you mention the word negligence to the Law Society and imply that your solicitor's idleness and incompetence has cost you money, the Law Society doesn't want to know. You might even get a letter back from them warning you that by writing such defamatory remarks about a respected member of the profession you could find yourself sued for libel. You will certainly receive a letter informing you that your only recourse is not to them but the law. But don't give up. You can still . . .

4. Complain to the legal ombudsman.

He handles complaints about solicitors that have been rejected by the Law Society.

As a Government appointment, he has the authority to question the Law Society and he must report back to the parties involved. But, alas, he has no power to force the Law Society to boot the scurrilous cad in the pants.

The ombudsman's official title is Lay Observer, and his name is Major-General J. G. R. Allen. Depending on his verdict, you may want to . . .

5. Sue a solicitor.

To sue a solicitor successfully you have to be able to prove that his negligence – rather than his bad judgement – has cost you money. For example, he might have let your case drag on so long that you find you can no longer continue with your case because the time limit has expired.

This, alas, is by no means uncommon, so much so that most solicitors now insure themselves against claims of negligence, which can cost them many thousands of pounds.

There is a catch, of course. To sue your solicitor you need a solicitor. And many firms are reluctant to do battle with fellow members of the profession with whom they may well have gone through law school. If you do have difficulty in finding a solicitor to take your case, write to your local Law Society or the Law Society in London, asking for a list of solicitors practising in your area, and then work your way down it until you find one who will oblige.

If you live outside London, it might be as well to find a solicitor who practises in London and who isn't quite so reluctant to upset his neighbours. Any Citizens' Advice Bureau will find a solicitor for you.

6. *Make a complaint to the police.*

If you suspect your solicitor of mishandling your funds, then it is a matter for the police just as much as if you caught a pickpocket with his hand on your wallet. Before shooting your mouth off about dishonesty, however, it is as well to be fairly sure of your suspicions and to consult another solicitor. Otherwise *you* could be the one who is sued – for slander.

If, understandably, you feel that you've had quite enough of solicitors, call in at your local police station and report all the facts to a CID officer, taking along any letters or papers that are relevant to the case.

7. *There is one other course of action open to a solicitor's dissatisfied client – that is to do nothing.*

Although this advice is strictly against the spirit and principles of this manual, when dealing with solicitors it is sometimes the winning way out.

You can often tell very early in the day that a solicitor is going to be no good to you – by the unreturned telephone calls, the unanswered letters, the difficulty in arranging appointments, the lack of familiarity with your case every time you see him.

To complain to the Law Society about him—successfully or otherwise – and then allow him to continue to look after your affairs, is not good psychology, and you are hardly likely to be buying the services of the devoted servant you badly need.

Best to ditch him for another solicitor before it's too late and pay him off with as little as you can get away with. NEVER refuse to pay a solicitor who has been handling a case for any length of time – he will simply hang on to your papers, as he is entitled to, until you come up with the money. Without the papers, no other solicitor is able to handle the case.

BARRISTERS

Barristers receive a great number of complaints about the way they handle their cases. Most of them come on writing paper rubber-stamped, H.M. PRISON, WORMWOOD SCRUBS.

Because most dissatisfied customers are unsuccessful litigants, barristers and their governing body, the Senate of the Inns of Court and the Bar, are not terribly sympathetic to complaints. If complaining about a solicitor is like going into the boxing ring with two hands tied behind your back, complaining about a barrister is like going into the ring bound hand and foot and blindfolded.

The first hurdle in this legalistic obstacle race is the Secretary of the Senate. Write to him with your allegations, and unless he reckons you're a raving nutcase, he will refer your complaint to the Professional Conduct Committee.

If the Committee considers there is evidence of conduct 'unbecoming a barrister' the President of the Senate will convene a disciplinary tribunal. Last year out of 179 complaints received by the Senate, more than half were rejected, fourteen barristers were 'admonished' like naughty school-

I HAVEN'T COME HERE TO ARGUE...

boys and fifteen were given 'a talking to'. That should teach them. Only fourteen were referred to a disciplinary tribunal and of these, five were disbarred, one was suspended and four were reprimanded.

The Senate is not interested in hearing about errors of judgement by barristers. They will only investigate what they term 'professional misconduct' or 'conduct unbecoming a barrister', although they are unhelpful about what this might be. There are no legal precedents for suing a barrister for an incompetent court performance.

If you feel you have been badly let down by a barrister due to his lack of care or diligence, you should certainly write to his Head of Chambers, whose name and address you will find in the Bar List at the Citizens' Advice Bureau or your local reference library.

You should also write to the Senate because, even if your complaint is a small one, it may be one of many received about the same barrister, and the Senate may feel it their duty to deliver a warning or a reprimand without referring it to the Professional Conduct Committee. They probably won't, though.

WARD'S LAW: The law is an asp.

LETTERS

The success or failure of a written complaint depends on two things:

1. Who you write to.
2. What you say and how you say it.

Let's get the name on the envelope right, first: Don't aim your first broadside too high. Henry Ford doesn't care two hoots about the horn button of your new car, and if you write to him about it, your letter will only be passed down the line until it gets to the one person who can do something about it – the service manager of your local garage.

He will understandably be peeved that you went over his head and, since the days of forelock-tugging are over, will probably do his utmost to make sure that your car breaks down again as soon as possible.

Your first letter should always be to the person immediately responsible for sorting out your problem – the service manager, the head buyer of the department (in the case of a large store), or the manager (of a small shop).

If that doesn't get you anywhere, then you can start writing to managing directors, chief executives and vice-presidents. But make sure you write to a name and not just a title. Letters addressed to 'The Managing Director' tend to be swiftly re-channelled without him ever seeing them, and you will spend the rest of your life corresponding with the area chief sales supervisor.

Type the letter, if at all possible. It's more business-like, and it saves the enemy struggling to read your scrawl.

Always keep a copy of the letters you write, and the replies you receive, as you may need to refer to them in the future.

What do you say and how do you say it?

If you have reason to complain, you can be pretty certain a lot of other customers are in the same boat. As your letter will be competing with theirs for sympathy and attention, it has to be good if it isn't to be relegated to the bottom of the pile.

Here are some valuable hints from a professional pain in the arse:

1. Make your letter easy to read by keeping the paragraphs short and being brief. I can't think of any letter of complaint that ought to be longer than ten paragraphs. Thus:

> *To: Mr R. Rotten-Timbers*
> *Managing Director*
> *The Nogood Building Co. Ltd*
>
> *No. 17 Dryrot Avenue*
>
> Dear Sir,
> *I write as the owner of the above property, purchased from you upon completion three weeks ago.*
> *Last night I returned home to discover that the house had completely collapsed, destroying all the contents.*
> *I would like to know your proposals for:*
> *1. Rebuilding the house.*
> *2. Rehousing, at your expense, me and my family until the new house is completed.*
> *3. Paying compensation for the damaged contents.*
> *Yours faithfully, etc.*

2. Always state the facts of your case clearly, providing dates, prices and names. Keep a diary of your discontent if necessary.

3. Your letter should put the ball firmly in the other

side's court. Don't just grumble about their inefficiency.
Tell them exactly what it is you want them to do to put
things right.

4. Never be angry or abusive. It only puts the other
person's back up and involves you in a slanging match.

5. When you are writing to the boss complaining about
the inefficiency of his staff, show yourself to be a reasonable
and patient person – with a sense of humour, even – who
has been tried beyond the limits of normal endurance. That
way, when his staff defensively tell him that you are a
'difficult customer', he'll believe you and not them.

6. Don't make a personal attack on the boss for the
shortcomings of his staff. You know it's his fault, he knows
it's his fault, but it doesn't help things to tell him. Question
his professionalism, by all means, but let him keep some professional pride, or you'll remind him of his ball-breaking wife.

7. Give the poor man room to manoeuvre. Don't put
him in a position where he would have to reverse completely

the decision of his senior executive to meet your demands. He has to feel he is backing up his staff, even if he isn't.

8. Resist the temptation to be a smart-arse. He's got a filing-cabinet full of letters whose last paragraphs end something like: 'Or am I to assume that it is the policy of your company that my wife and I should spend the remainder of our married life cooking over an open fire in the garden?' The final sneer antagonizes, without adding anything to your argument.

That's enough theorizing. Now for some examples. The following letters all achieved their objective within a week of their receipt. Only the names have been changed to protect the guilty.

To: Mr I. L. Cockitup
Managing Director
Solutions Unlimited Ltd

Dear Sir,
I understand that the function of your organization was to provide solutions to your clients' problems, not to create new problems.

This is the record of the simple operation of wall-papering my kitchen:

Wednesday, 19 June. An appointment is made to meet a representative of the decorators at my flat. He does not, however, turn up.

Thursday, 20 June. A new appointment is made, the representative arrives and undertakes to start the work on Monday and complete it in two days.

Friday, 28 June. I arrive back from holiday to find only one wall papered, and an incoherent note, written on the back of a piece of wallpaper, to the effect that the decorators have been given the wrong paper by the suppliers. The note contains a promise to turn up on Saturday and complete the work.

Saturday, 29 June. The decorators' representative turns up with a workman. Having apologized for the inconvenience he departs, but omits to leave my only spare set of keys with the workman, with the result that someone has to remain in the flat to let the workman in and out. The workman does not complete the work as promised for the reason that he did not start until after 11 am. He undertakes to come back on Monday and finish the work.

Monday, 1 July. He does not turn up.

Tuesday, 2 July. Still no sign of him. I am told that he cannot come until tomorrow. Meanwhile, the decorators' representative is wandering around London with my keys in his pocket.

There, at the moment, the matter rests. After repeated protest to you I have now been told that this work will be finished this afternoon. I will believe this when I see it.

Yours faithfully, etc.

*   *   *

To: Mr A. P. Alling
Managing Director
The Fraud Motor Co.

Dear Sir,

My WoW 2000GT has been off the road for four weeks now because your stores have been out of exhaust systems.

I find it extraordinary that such rudimentary spare parts should ever be allowed to be out of stock, and I am sure this is not your intention. The WoW 2000GT is a fine car, but it is also an expensive car with expensive spare parts, and I think it is reasonable to expect an after-sales service to match its performance and price.

Auto-Crash car service, who are understandably fed up with garaging my immobile car, tell me that unhappily my

*experience is not a unique one. They have three other customers'
WoW 2000GTs similarly immobilized.*

*Besides the inconvenience of being without my own car I
have already spent nearly £140 on hiring a replacement. This
in addition to a fairly hefty repair bill I have to pay if and when
I get my car back.*

Please can you give this your urgent attention?

Yours faithfully, etc.

*   *   *

To: Mr Frank Foam
Managing Director
Floodedout Washing Machine Sales Co. Ltd

Dear Sir,

On 14 November I purchased from you a Sudsimatic 500
washing machine, price £254.50.

On 18 November, the coil of the motor burned out and I
was without the use of the machine for two weeks until a
replacement motor could be fitted under guarantee; on 6 December the machine broke down again, due to a faulty fly-wheel;
on 12 December, it was out of action for a further week when
the switch-panel fused.

I was assured by your chief service engineer, Mr Perry,
that these were merely 'unlucky teething troubles' but today the
five-week-old machine (of which I have had less than three
weeks' use) flooded my kitchen, ruining a rug and damaging the
floor tiles.

As you know, under the Sale of Goods Act, goods offered
for sale have to be of merchantable quality and fit for the
purpose for which they are intended.

It is my contention that because of these frequent breakdowns this machine is neither fit for its intended purpose, nor

was it of merchantable quality when I bought it. Nevertheless I am going to let you have one last attempt at putting it right.

Unless, however, it is repaired to my complete satisfaction within seven days and continues to give good service thereafter, I will cancel the purchase and ask you to return the full purchase price.

In the circumstances I must also ask you to recompense me for the damage caused by the machine flooding, namely the cleaning of a rug and the re-cementing of the floor tiles.

Yours faithfully, etc.

*   *   *

To: Mr Rodney Gasbag
Service Manager
The South-East Incompetence Gas Board

COPY: District Manager, South-East Incompetence
*   Gas Board*
*   Chairman, South-East Incompetence Gas*
*   Consumers' Council*
*   Mr Fred Talkalot, MP*

Dear Sir,
During the past week I have made five telephone calls to your service department asking for a fitter to call to repair my hot-water geyser. Five appointments have been made, five appointments broken.

I do not seek an explanation for this unforgivable inefficiency and discourtesy. I simply want a fitter to call so that we can once again enjoy the service for which we are paying.

I would be grateful if you or your deputy could telephone me at once to arrange an appointment that, this time, will be kept.

Yours faithfully, etc.

*   *   *

To: Mr A. Robot
Data Processing Manager
The Sillybugger Manufacturing Co. Ltd

COPY: Mr Arnold Countalot, Chief Accountant
       Mr Michael Illinformed, Managing Director

Dear Sir,
    I wonder if you could have a word with your computer about the enclosed account?
    I have written several times to the Accounts Department pointing out that this bill has been paid, but, of course, they do not have the computer's ear, as you do.
    It would be a pity if your computer felt obliged to sue me, as it obviously intends to, mistakenly believing that I was in debt.
    May I leave this matter in your capable (electronic) hands?
    Yours faithfully, etc.

You will notice that copies of the last two letters were sent to other interested parties. It's a good way, this, of attacking on two fronts while covering yourself.

Most large organizations are torn apart by inter-office rivalry and bitchery, and by unleashing dog against dog, you increase your chances of getting your problem solved by someone who has his own interests at heart. A sales manager is much more likely to act promptly if he knows that the managing director has been informed – although not bothered – about your complaint.

WARD'S LAW: Someone, somewhere, deserves a nasty letter from you.

MAIL ORDER

Mail-order shoppers enjoy exactly the same protection in law as the person who walks into a shop (see 'Shops' and 'Trade Descriptions Act'). The most frequently heard complaint about mail-order firms, however, is that they don't deliver the goods – or they take six months to do so, during which time they have the interest-free use of your money.

If this happens, send a letter by recorded delivery insisting that unless they deliver, or refund your money within seven days, you will report them to the Advertising Standards Authority and sue them. (Once you have set a date by which you must have the goods, you don't have to accept them if they arrive after your deadline.)

If that doesn't evoke a reply, write to the Advertising Standards Authority giving all the details of the original advertisement, when you sent off the money, etc. They will investigate your complaint and may prevent the firm from placing any further advertisements until it meets its commitments.

Write the same letter to the Advertising Manager of the newspaper or magazine in which you saw the offer and ask him to pursue the matter for you.

If you've been conned – it does happen with fly-by-night mail-order crooks from time to time – you should also get in touch with the police.

If the mail-order firm goes bankrupt, you can now recover your money from a 'disaster fund' set up by the Newspaper Publishers' Association – provided that the paper or magazine is a member.

WARD'S LAW: Don't be beaten by the loneliness of the long-distance complainer.

THE MANAGEMENT CANNOT BE HELD RESPONSIBLE . . .

That's what the sign says, all right, but it's wrong. The management CAN be held responsible. Under the Unfair Contract Terms Act, firms can't duck out of their responsibilities simply by sticking a disclaimer notice on the wall.

Signs rejecting liability for death or injury have no effect in law and you can ignore them. Other disclaimers – in dry-cleaning shops, cloakrooms, garages, etc. – won't protect the management from claims for compensation, provided that you can prove that the loss or damage was caused by the firm's negligence. (See 'Small Print'.)

I SPEAK YOUR WEIGHT

I'M SAYING NOTHING TILL I'VE SPOKEN TO THE FIRM'S LAWYERS..

MINISTRY OF WEIGHTS AND MEASURES

Despite their rights or wrongs in law, 'Management Cannot' signs do, however, tell you one thing: just what kind of a management you're dealing with. For this reason only, they're worth a careful inspection.

WARD'S LAW: The management is *irresponsible*.

HOW TO LOBBY
YOUR MP

Your MP can be your biggest ally in your fight against injustice or bureaucracy, and you don't even have to have voted for him.

When an MP writes to a Minister about your problem, the letter goes directly to that Minister, by-passing the hundreds of civil servants en route.

When YOU write to a Minister, the letter goes into the civil-service machinery and it may be weeks before the Minister ever sees it – if he sees it at all.

MPs are used to helping their constituents with every kind of problem, but obviously they can bring more pressure to bear when a Government department or local authority is involved. You would be amazed how many backsides can be shifted by a letter on House of Commons writing paper. An MP might even raise your case in Parliament.

How can you successfully lobby your MP?

First of all you have to find out who he – or she – is. Ring your Town Hall or Citizens' Advice Bureau, tell them where you live and ask who your MP is. Also ask for the address and telephone number of the MP's constituency office.

Write to your MP there, or at the House of Commons (if Parliament is sitting), explaining your problem as briefly as possible and asking for an appointment.

MPs hold 'surgeries' in their constituencies about once

a month when people with problems can come along and talk to them. Take along with you all the facts and correspondence relevant to your case so that you can sort things out there and then.

Don't be afraid to bother an MP – that's what they're there for. You would be surprised how often an MP says to a constituent, 'For heaven's sake, why didn't you come to me before?'

There's nothing to stop you just calling in to see him or her at the House of Commons, of course, though it's a bit of a hit-and-miss business. MPs, like schoolteachers, spend half their life on holiday, so find out first if Parliament is sitting. Have a look in your newspaper to see if proceedings in Parliament are being reported, or call the Serjeant at Arms at the Commons, telephone number 01-219 3000.

Tell the policeman on the gate in Parliament Square that you want to see your MP and he will direct you to the Central Lobby where you can fill out a green card requesting an audience.

A messenger then sets out in search of your MP. Be prepared for a long wait. He might not be there at all that day. He might be involved in an important debate in the Chamber and not be able to get out for an hour or so. More likely he will be in the Members' Bar.

London MPs get called on quite frequently by their constituents and are therefore less likely to drop whatever they are doing to come out to see you. But if you live a long way from London, it is an unfriendly MP indeed who won't see a constituent when he is at the House.

The best time to get him is probably between 3 pm and 8 pm.

What happens if your MP is an idle no-good who isn't interested in you or your problems?

Then find another MP who *is*. MPs are, by their very nature, interfering busybodies and there is bound to be one who wishes to make your crusade his victory. MPs have a variety of interests and these are systematically listed in an informative volume called *Cassell's Parliamentary Directory* by Malcolm Hulke. Having trouble with your bees or allotment? Mr Hulke knows an MP who is longing to swop stories about your mutual hobby.

If you can't find a sympathetic ear, find out who the MP in the next-door constituency is. If he belongs to the same party as your MP tell him that you know that, strictly speaking, he shouldn't see you, but that you haven't had much success interesting Mr So-and-so with your problem and would he mind sparing you five minutes of his important time. I don't promise anything, but with a good MP it should work.

Can anyone in the House of Lords help?

Peers are an underworked and often willing body of influential men and women. A letter to a Government department from a Peer carries almost as much weight as a letter from an MP, and there is probably more chance of your problem being given an airing in the House of Lords.

Peers support many different campaigns; Baroness Burton, for instance, is a tireless champion of consumer rights. So don't forget our Lords and Mistresses.

WARD'S LAW: A victory for you is another vote for your MP.

MOTORISTS

Pedestrians hate motorists, parking wardens hate motorists, even other motorists hate motorists. Does no one love motorists? No one at all, I am afraid, except the people who make and maintain their silly cars.

How can you do the dirty on a motorist?

Fortunately, drivers themselves make this all too easy by constantly breaking the law.

You simply book them as any policeman would. Ask Lord Snowdon. He was booked for careless driving and later found guilty and fined, entirely as the result of a complaint by another motorist.

What should you do if you meet a motoring maniac?

Say a driver has just attempted to run you down on a zebra crossing or has recklessly overtaken you on the inside at 90 mph on the M1.

Take the registration number of the car, the name and address of the driver (if he stops) and get the names of as many friendly witnesses as possible – your passengers, passers-by, other motorists, etc. You then go to the police station nearest to where the offence was committed and tell them you wish to prosecute this maniac.

After listening to your boring story, the police will then decide whether:

(a) *To prosecute your would-be assassin.*
(b) *To forget the whole thing and go back to sleep.*
(c) *To prosecute YOU for dangerous driving.*

If they decide there are grounds for prosecuting the other driver, all your troubles are over and the other driver's are just beginning. The police will take over the prosecution, just as if they themselves had witnessed the offence being committed. You will be called as a witness.

If, on the other hand, they decide they've had enough paperwork for one week, all is not lost. You can still take out a *private* summons against the driver. Go to the magistrates' court nearest to the scene of the incident and tell the clerk to the court all the relevant facts. He will help you.

This is what photographer Ray Bellisario did (successfully) after Lord Snowdon reversed into him. But be warned. It is likely to involve you in a lot of work and expense, and without the help of a solicitor only an aggressor bent on revenge should attempt this perilous course.

First of all, you may still not know the name of the driver you wish to prosecute.

You can find out who is the registered owner of the maniac car by writing to the Driver and Vehicle Licensing Centre at Swansea. You have to satisfy the DVLC that you have 'reasonable cause' to have access to the identity of the owner, and you will have to pay a £2 search fee.

You should write off to Swansea immediately because,

depending on what the charge is, you may have to serve
notice of intended prosecution on the driver within fourteen
days of the alleged offence. The clerk of the court will also
help you do this.

*You've done your bit as Dixon of Dock Green – now's your
chance to try your luck as Perry Mason.*

The court will issue the actual summons, but when the
case comes up you (or your solicitor) will have to put the
prosecution case.

The way is strewn with pitfalls and, if you lose, you
could be landed with not only your own costs but also the
expenses of the bloke you were out to get. A double defeat!
The villain may even sue you – for malicious prosecution.

*What can you do about the motorist who selfishly obstructs
your garage exit or blocks your car in by parking badly?*

Well, you can ring the police and report that there's a
car obstructing the highway and ask them to tow it away.
(Due to a bizarre oversight in the law, no one has the right
to park anywhere, except, perhaps, in their own sitting-
room.)

But sometimes justice is swifter and sweeter through less
official (and illegal) channels. All drivers are in love with their
cars, and by getting at their loved one, you strike deep at
their very hearts.

A threat should do the trick. A driver who fears he will
return to find his car tyres deflated will choose his parking
place with great consideration for other road-users.

**WARD'S LAW: Prosecute a motorist and help
keep death off the roads.**

NEIGHBOURS

Neighbours, like relatives, cannot – alas – be chosen. Whether you like them or not, you've got them until one or other of you obligingly moves or dies.

I wouldn't go so far as to suggest that you should love your neighbours, but if you can get on with them it helps. Conflicts are bound to crop up from time to time and a quiet word over the fence is on the whole preferable to a six-week High Court action.

If you're unlucky enough to have bolshy neighbours, however, there are ways to settle most disputes besides punching them on the nose, or selling up.

The key word in settling all neighbour disputes is *reasonable*. If your neighbour is acting *unreasonably* then you might be able to bring an action for nuisance against him in the magistrates' court.

It's *reasonable* for your neighbour to saw up wood in the garden a couple of times a week, but it's *unreasonable* if he sets up a small sawmill business at the bottom of the garden.

It's *reasonable* to burn leaves and grass in the garden, but *unreasonable* to have an incinerator belching thick black smoke every day.

It's *reasonable* that he should repair his car when it goes wrong, but *unreasonable* to take it upon himself to build a yacht in his back garden so that you don't get any peace at weekends for four years.

It is no defence to say that the nuisance existed before you moved in.

The law protects you from your neighbours' more eccentric and unsightly building extensions, too.

Is it a blot on your landscape?

If planning permission hasn't been obtained, you might be able to prevent an eyesore on environmental grounds.

Does it violate your privacy?

If a balcony gave your neighbour a clear view into your bedroom window, for instance, you would probably be able to obtain an order getting him to take it down – though you won't if the balcony overlooks only your garden.

Does it block out your light?

Any window that has had uninterrupted light for 21 years is entitled to keep it, under an old law called Ancient Lights.

If any of these problems are your problems, then you should get in touch with the planning department of your local council. And the sooner the better.

Neighbours' animals probably cause more trouble than their owners. Dogs that run wild and trample down flowers, or that bark a lot, could be committing a nuisance under the Animals Act. An animal doesn't have to be very big to be considered a nuisance, either. If your neighbour's hamsters started seeking asylum in your bedroom, or stank the place out, they would be declared a public menace.

And, just as your neighbour owes it to you to keep his pets under control, so he has to keep overhanging bushes and trees off your property, too. If he doesn't trim them back after a couple of polite requests, you can do it for him.

WARD'S LAW: Love thy neighbour, and if that doesn't work, give him hell.

NEWSPAPERS

There is one subject that few people like to read about in a newspaper – themselves.

It didn't happen like that at all, you see. They're fifty-three, not fifty-four. They never said that. And, anyway, what business is it of the newspaper *what* they did or said?

It's an all-too-familiar story for every newspaper editor, I am afraid.

No one is perfect, but when newspapers make a mistake, it's there for millions to read, to the lasting embarrassment of you, the victim. And when they *do* boob at your expense, you deserve an apology and a correction published.

What should you do if you feel that a newspaper or one of its reporters or photographers has given you a hard time?

Well, if you think you may have been libelled – a fairly rare event since all newspapers employ teams of legal advisers at vast expense – you should see a solicitor. DON'T write to the editor, because you might easily say the wrong thing and ruin your subsequent chances of suing the paper successfully.

(Few libel cases ever get to court. Newspapers generally know when they're in the wrong and prefer to settle out of court.)

Most likely, however, there has been what we in the newspaper business commonly call a cock-up. A reporter has got his facts wrong or exaggerated a bit to make it 'a good story'; or a sub-editor has made a mistake when re-writing a reporter's story; or the headline bears little relation to the story that follows underneath it.

Whatever it is, unless you intend to sue for libel, the first thing you must do is write to the editor. You'll find the address somewhere in the newspaper, usually at the bottom of the back page.

Editors are responsible men who take their jobs seriously and they don't like it when the paper slips up. If a mistake has been made, or you have reasonable grounds for complaint, someone's arse will be kicked, I can assure you.

But as the harm has already been done, the problem is: Will you get a printed apology? Editors are reluctant to print corrections unless they absolutely have to, partly because it undermines readers' confidence in the newspaper and partly because there wouldn't be room for any news if they printed a correction to every mistake they made. So if it's a minor mistake, you really don't have a chance.

Even if it's a serious error, the editor won't volunteer to print a correction unless you insist, and that is what you must do.

When a newspaper describes you as 'unemployed, crippled and elderly' when you are employed, perfectly sound in body and limb and only forty-five years old, they have, after all, a moral obligation to correct the wrong impression they caused.

What can you do if the editor refuses to budge?

You can take it up with one of his superiors. All newspapers have a Chairman and most have an Editorial Director, who is a supremo above all the editors in that newspaper group. But they will probably back their editor. And if they do, the only course left to you is –

TO COMPLAIN TO THE PRESS COUNCIL.

The Press Council is an independent watchdog set up in 1953 to look into complaints against newspapers and magazines, and to make sure they maintain 'the highest professional standards'. It consists of a thirty-seven-strong committee, eighteen of whom are lay members with no connections with the Press.

The Council will investigate allegations of misreporting, intrusion, hounding, foot-in-the-door and other sharp practices by reporters and photographers. Any reader can complain to the Council about an article or picture they consider to be in bad taste, even if they are in no way involved personally.

After investigating a complaint, the Press Council issues an 'adjudication' either condemning the newspaper or rejecting the complaint, and the newspaper has to publish the findings if they are critical of the publication. It's no more than a high-level rap over the knuckles, but a condemnation reflects badly on an editor and his paper.

To complain to the Press Council write to the Director

saying you would like your complaint to be considered by
the Complaints Committee and enclose:

1. *A dated cutting of the article or picture in question.*
2. *A copy of any correspondence with the editor.*
3. *If you are complaining about being misquoted, a signed
   statement by any witness who can support your case.*

The Director will prepare a dossier of your complaint
and invite the editor and reporter/photographer involved to
make a statement giving their side of the story. They might
even ask the reporter to produce his notebook, if his notes
at the time are relevant to the case.

Your complaint then goes before a Complaints Committee of thirteen members (six of them lay members) who
meet twice a month under the Chairman, Mr Patrick Neill,
QC.

You may be asked to give evidence before the Committee. Or the editor may exercise his right to appear
personally, in which case you will also have the opportunity
to come along.

In cases of intrusion or invasion of privacy, the editor
will probably defend his actions by telling the Committee
that he considered it to be 'in the public interest'. If there
were serious inaccuracies in a story and no correction or
apology was subsequently published, it would obviously
count against him.

After sifting through all the facts, the Complaints
Committee will do one of four things:

1. *Call for further evidence*
2. *Declare that your complaint is of 'insufficient substance
   to warrant an adjudication', and chuck it out.*
3. *Recommend an adjudication to the full Press Council
   rejecting your complaint.*
4. *Recommend an adjudication to the full Press Council
   upholding your complaint.*

In the event of decision *3* or *4*, the Council of thirty-seven, which meets every two months, will then reconsider all the evidence. Usually it goes along with the adjudication recommended by the Complaints Committee, but it has the power to reverse or vary it, and occasionally does so.

You *can't* make a complaint to the Press Council and then sue a newspaper afterwards, by the way. If there is the slightest possibility of a civil court action resulting from the cause of your complaint, you will be asked to sign a form waiving all your rights in law against the newspaper.

This might seem sinister, but there are good reasons:

1. *The Press Council doesn't want to be used by prospective litigants to 'try out' their case on the cheap.*
2. *No editor would give evidence before the Press Council if he thought it might subsequently damage his paper's chances in a libel action.*

There is nothing to stop you suing first and then complaining to the Press Council afterwards, however.

Just *threatening* to complain to the Press Council is quite a big stick to beat editors with if you really feel you are owed an apology and a correction. There's nothing to stop you lodging a complaint with the Press Council and then writing to the editor offering to withdraw it if he publishes a correction.

As a journalist I am only too accustomed to receiving complaints. I have one here, as a matter of fact. 'Dear Mr Ward,' it says. 'Re your column last week. Why don't you get stuffed? Yours sincerely, Very Bored, Bournemouth.'

If only all our readers were so easy to please.

WARD'S LAW: Don't be eaten alive by newspaper tigers.

NOISE

Have you noticed how noisy life has become these days? I SAID HAVE YOU NOTICED HOW NOISY LIFE HAS BECOME THESE DAYS?

In this imperfect world you may not, alas, ever be able to find complete silence, but you can at least succeed in turning down the volume a little.

Noisy neighbours, transistors on the beach, pile-drivers at night, barking dogs . . . you can legally silence all of these nervous-breakdown-inducing nuisances, leaving you completely undisturbed to listen to the roar of passing lorries and low-flying aircraft.

How do you shut up a persistently noisy neighbour?

Well, yes, you can always bang on the ceiling with a broomstick handle or play Mahler's 4th symphony with the windows open at 3 am – but you could be the one to end up in court for disturbing *them*.

In law there are three courses of action open to you:

1. Under Common Law you can ask a solicitor to apply to a judge in chambers for an injunction to stop the noise, provided that it is 'materially interfering with your comfort'. It's a very expensive way of buying peace, this.
2. You yourself can instigate a prosecution at your local magistrates' court under the Control of Pollution Act, 1974. The Clerk of the Court will help you prepare an application for a Noise Abatement Notice, as it's called.

3. You can report the nuisance to the Environmental Health Officer at the Town Hall. Local authorities are responsible for administering the Control of Pollution Act, and because noise so often affects health, the Health Officer is the person to see. Some councils even have a Noise Control Officer.

Of these three, the last is probably the best course. A court case would be costly and time-consuming if the enemy stubbornly defends the case. Court cases also tend to leave behind a tide-mark of ill feeling which could cause you more trouble than the original nuisance.

The intervention of the Environmental Health Officer, on the other hand, could remove the nuisance without the matter ever having to come to court. And if the noise persists, then the council will do the prosecuting, saving you the trouble and expense.

What noises can you shut up?

Almost any row that causes *unreasonable* disturbance – even the noisy love-making of the couple upstairs.

The time that the noise is made can be a key factor when the court comes to decide whether or not it constitutes a nuisance. Pile-driving during daylight hours, for instance, is regarded as necessary on a building site and therefore reasonable; pile-driving at night, however, is unreasonable and therefore can be stopped.

Even nature is not beyond the law: a dawn chorus of cockerels is not grounds for an action in itself; but if it continues for weeks in a residential area, you would get an injunction and damages.

What about barking dogs and transistor radios on the beach?

Obviously you can't go running off barefoot in your swimming trunks to the Town Hall to sneak to the Environmental Health Officer.

Mercifully, most boroughs have bye-laws prohibiting noisy animals and the playing of radios, etc. in public places, so ask the person responsible for the row to belt up – and if that doesn't produce results, call the police and tell them that the noisy lout's behaviour is about to provoke a breach of the peace.

Complaints about TV and radio interference caused by neighbours' cars and power drills not fitted with suppressors, should be addressed to the Post Office, who have powers to order the fitting of suppressors. It's as well to first check you've got a licence, though.

Typically, the biggest noise nuisance of all – aircraft noise – is not covered by the Control of Pollution Act. The only thing you can do is get some signatures together and lobby your MP in the hope of getting flight paths changed. Representations should also be made in the form of frequent letters and telephone calls to the British Airports Authority office at the airport they are flying to or from.

The Department of Trade also has a special section that deals with complaints about aircraft noise. This section has the magnificent title of CA3/3 and is installed, conveniently distant from Heathrow Airport, at: Civil Aviation Division, Department of Trade, 7 Victoria Street, London SW1.

The Noise Abatement Society, a voluntary organization that has done much to reduce our daily decibel intake, will help you fight any noise battle. Write to them giving full details of your problem and what, if any, steps you have already taken.

They charge £6 for their expert advice (£5 for members). It's cheaper than consulting a solicitor, anyway. They will also put you in touch with a professional acoustics consultant who, for a fee, will gather any necessary scientific evidence you need to win your case, and give evidence for you in court. In no time at all, you'll be able to sleep peacefully again.

I SAID IN NO TIME AT ALL YOU'LL BE ABLE TO SLEEP PEACEFULLY AGAIN.

WARD'S LAW: Noise annoys.

PASSING THE BUCK

The least-spoken words in the English language are: *'I'm terribly sorry, it's entirely my fault.'* In fact, this might be the first time these words have ever been written.

No one ever accepts the blame when something goes wrong. It has always been Someone Else's Fault and it will always be Someone Else's Fault.

For instance, when a motor mechanic opens your car bonnet and says, 'What idiot has been mucking around in here?' he is merely looking for someone else to blame for something he hasn't even done yet.

The well-practised art of blaming someone else is known as passing the buck. It is a technique used by the guilty to drive you mad while they escape scot-free. What happens is this.

Let's say, for the sake of argument, that you have been waiting seven years, three months and four days for a replacement table leg for your Swedish kitchen table. You're suddenly fed up with having to eat with one hand while holding up the table with the other hand, and you go storming round to the shop where you ordered the replacement leg.

The shopkeeper throws his hands in the air in despair. 'It's those damned importers,' he says, 'if you can make them pull their finger out, you'd be doing me a favour.'

So you get on to the importers. 'I don't know what's taking the shipping line so long,' they say. 'Perhaps *you* would like to have a word with them. I'm sick of telephoning them.'

The shipper says: 'We can't transport goods we were

never given in the first place. Those Swedes obviously forgot to process the order at the factory. Why don't you tear them off a strip? They'll listen to someone like you.'

But the Swedes say your table leg was sent off five years ago. 'Obviously your Customs are holding it. We suggest . . .'

By this time you have had to give up your job to devote more time to the investigation. Your house – along with the three-legged kitchen table – has been sold to finance your trips and telephone calls to Sweden. Your wife leaves you and finally you are taken away screaming to a funny farm after being found guilty of sawing the legs off 143 tables belonging to other people.

Town halls and Government departments are infested with buck-passers who shunt you from extension to extension, department to department, until your resistance is worn down.

One way of beating a buck-passer is to turn the tables on him by setting dog against dog. Ask him to put in writing whose fault he considers it to be. Send his letter to the person he is accusing – and let them fight it out between them. It doesn't produce any results for you, but it's an entertaining sport.

A more effective tactic is this: right at the beginning you

say, 'I don't care whose fault it is, I'm holding you responsible.' You then get them by the throat and make their life a misery until you get what you want.

They'll never take the blame, but they might take the responsibility.

WARD'S LAW: Find a name, fix the blame.

POLICE

More than sore feet, more than a National Front demo, more even than point duty in the rain, a policeman dreads to hear the words, 'Section 49'.

Section 49 of the Police Act, 1949, is the law under which a policeman can be prosecuted or disciplined for misconduct.

What does a policeman have to do to be guilty of a breach of discipline?

Almost anything, poor chap. The police code of conduct is even stricter than army discipline and does not make any allowances for the fact that policemen are, after all, human like the rest of us.

Although there are 1001 things a policeman can do wrong during an eight-hour shift, all complaints against the police can be roughly divided into two groups – major and minor.

1. MAJOR: Any allegation of a criminal offence – that is to say, bribery or corruption, planting evidence, perjury, assault, etc.
2. MINOR: Lapses that can be dealt with by internal discipline such as incivility, swearing, ignoring a request for help, harassment, etc.

Because the police force expects its officers to be beyond reproach, the procedure for making an official complaint is exactly the same however trivial the allegation.

This is what you do

1. Write to the Chief Constable (or, in the case of the Metropolitan or City of London Police, to the Police Commissioner at New Scotland Yard) giving details of your complaint. *Or*

2. Call at any police station. Say you wish to make a complaint and would like to see a senior officer to make a statement. (Don't be surprised if they don't all fall at your feet though.) If there isn't a senior officer there, ask for an appointment to see one, or to be visited at home by one. You might also ask for a Home Office pamphlet, *Police And Public*, which gives the procedure for making a complaint. If they haven't got one, they ought to, and you should complain about that, too.

This is what happens

A vast, cumbersome but thorough piece of investigative machinery clanks into action.

1. Your complaint is – has to be – immediately recorded in a book.

2. An Investigating Officer of a rank not less than Chief Inspector is appointed to look into your complaint. He must be from a different division to the officer under suspicion and, in the case of serious complaints, may even be from a different police force.

3. He will interview you, ask you questions, and take a statement from you.

4. The policeman (or policemen) concerned will be given 'Form 163' which informs him that he is the subject of an investigation and outlines the allegations against him.

5. He is then interviewed by the Investigating Officer and asked for his side of the story.

6. The Investigating Officer sends his report to the Deputy Chief Constable.

7. The Deputy Chief Constable now has all the facts and will do one of three things:

(a) *If the report suggests that the officer might have broken the law, the papers will be sent to the Director of Public Prosecutions who will decide whether or not to institute criminal proceedings. If your complaint does result in a court case, you will have to appear as a witness, of course.*

(b) *If the Deputy Chief Constable feels instead there has been a serious breach of discipline (I imagine this would include entertaining ladies of ill repute in the back of a police car) he will bring disciplinary charges against the police officer. This is a police version of a court martial. The allegations might be heard by the Chief Constable, sitting alone as judge and jury, or a tribunal might be set up with two senior police officers and two members of the independent Police Complaints Board. You will be called to say your piece, but afterwards you will be told only the result of the hearing – not what the punishment was – if the result went against the copper. He might be reprimanded, cautioned, reduced in pay or rank, asked to resign or be dismissed. You'll never have the satisfaction of knowing.*

(c) *If the Deputy Chief Constable decides you are making a fuss about nothing, and that there is no need for disciplinary action, things don't end there. The original Investigating Officer's report is sent to the Police Complaints Board who will consider all the facts and might order the Deputy Chief Constable to bring charges after all.*

As you can see, it's a pretty complicated and time-consuming procedure. Unless a copper has behaved fairly appallingly, I really wouldn't bother if I were you. There's no point in having a police force that's so busy investigating complaints against itself that it doesn't have time to get on with its job.

And as it is often only your word against a policeman's, and he'll deny it (if he's got any sense he will, anyway), your complaint will probably fail.

An awful lot do. In 1978 the Police Complaints Board, headed by Lord Plowden, considered more than thirteen thousand complaints. Only FIFTEEN resulted in 'disciplinary action' and about 1,000 led to the police officer concerned being 'the subject of advice' – in other words, told not to do it again.

Is there any other way you can register your displeasure? Officially, no. Unofficially, yes. You could always tell the policeman concerned that you *are* filing a complaint against him under Section 49, even if you have no intention of doing so. The fact that you even know the words will certainly spoil his appetite for supper that night and might even make him think twice next time.

Or, if your fight is with a constable or detective constable, you might try having a quiet word with his senior officer. Call round at the police station and ask to speak to the station sergeant or the duty officer. Say something like, 'Look, I don't want to make anything of this under Section 49, but you might have a word with that PC 37 of yours, who just told me to f*** off.'

The sergeant's boot will soon be winging its way towards the seat you yourself would have liked to kick, but for which you would have been given six months.

WARD'S LAW: All policemen are guilty until proven innocent.

POST OFFICE

TELEPHONES

One of the biggest obstacles in the way of the telephone subscriber who wishes to make an effective complaint is . . . well, the telephone.

'Hello, is that Engineers? This is 01-246 8070. Can you please do something about the terrible crackling on my line? I . . .'

'*I'm sorry, Sir, I can't hear you. There's a terrible crackling on the line. Will you replace your receiver and call back please?*'

OR:

'Hello, is that Sales? This is Mr Ward here. I was wondering when you were going to install my telephone. It's been two months now and . . .'

'*The matter is in hand, Mr Ward. We'll call you as soon as an engineer is free and fix an appointment.*'

'How can you call me when I haven't got a telephone?'

'*But you're talking on the phone now.*'

'I'm in a call box.'

'*You have my word, Mr Ward. I'll call you as soon as I know anything. What's your number again?*'

The other mistake we subscribers make is to imagine that there really is a Telephone Manager in the 'Telephone Manager's Office', the number of which is so brazenly printed across our telephone bills.

I once had this conversation with my local Telephone Manager's office:

'Hello. Is that the Telephone Manager's Office?'
(Woman's voice): '*It is.*'
'May I speak to the Telephone Manager, please?'
'*I'm afraid he's not here just now.*'
'Who am I speaking to?'
'*I'm the cleaner.*'

There's no shortage of people in the Telephone
Manager's Office, though none of them will ever admit to
being the Telephone Manager. Some of them, however, can
help you with your problems. Whenever possible, get the
person's name and title, so that you don't have to repeat your
complaint to someone new each time.

PROBLEM	ASK FOR
Rudeness, or Operator takes hours to answer	Service Manager
Telephone persistently out of order/crossed lines, etc., despite repeated calls to engineers	Area Engineer
Query over bill	Area Accountant
New telephone installations or alterations to existing equipment	Sales and Installation Manager

The man in charge of the whole shooting match (or
perhaps I should say shouting match) is the General Manager
– the title Telephone Manager doesn't exist any more,
although it is still widely and wrongly used.

If you can somehow trick the switchboard into revealing
his name (pretending you're from the Post Office newspaper,
Courier, always works, I find) you've got a chance of getting
through to him. Call back and ask for him by name – and say
it's a personal call. Otherwise you'll have to write.

But General Managers in their turn have above them a
big white chief in the form of a Regional Director. London

has no less than eleven General Managers, for instance, but only one Regional Director. He hangs out at Post Office London Telecommunications Region, Camelford House, 87/90 Albert Embankment, London, SE1 7TS.

There are ten Regional Directors in Britain and you can find out the address of yours by ringing up the General Manager's office and asking for 'the address of the Regional Directorate for this telecommunications region'. It might be 150 miles away, but don't be put off. That is where the strings are pulled from.

Alternatively, if you find you're getting nowhere locally you might want to take your problem straight to the top. Sir William Barlow is Chairman of the Post Office and can be contacted at Post Office Headquarters, 23 Howland Street, London W1. His Managing Director (Telecommunications) is Mr Peter Benton at Post Office Headquarters, 2 Gresham Street, London EC2V 7AG.

POST
The hierarchy structure of the postal side of the Post Office is very similar in many ways to the telephone system's.

Starting at the top this time:

The Big Chief Supremo Postmaster is of course our old friend Sir William. Under him comes the Managing Director (Postal) Mr Denis Roberts at Postal Headquarters, St Martins-le-Grand, London EC1. Try not to bother either of these two about your auntie's birthday card taking two days to travel from London to Bournemouth.

Under these two are nine Regional Directors, each responsible for their own particular area of the country. You can find out where your Regional Director is by ringing or calling at your local Postal headquarters and asking for the address of 'the Regional Directorate for this postal region'.

Regional Directors have several Head Postmasters under them, each one in charge of his own 'patch'. London, being rather more concentrated than, say, Little Nuttingford, has in addition District Postmasters with Assistant District Postmasters under them.

So a good rule is: in London, write to the District Postmaster of your area. Outside, write to the Head Postmaster for the area. And if that doesn't get you anywhere go to your Regional Director, and let him sort it out.

Postmasters and the like are anonymous bureaucrats who try not to be seen by the public. But at every Post Office there is an Officer in Charge whom you can insist on talking to if you run into trouble with rude or unhelpful counter clerks.

If you don't want to involve yourself with the Post Office's hierarchy structure, you can inject yourself right into its complaints system. London has two 'customer relations officers' whose job it is to investigate and sort out complaints. Outside London, all regions have 'public relations officers' to pacify angry post and telephone customers.

Who else can help you in your battle with the Post Office?

Well, there's POUNC, the Post Office Users' National Council, an independent watchdog body that periodically bashes the Post Office on behalf of the public. It's not interested in sorting out your private squabbles, but it will weigh in on your side in matters of public interest – long delays in telephone installation if you are a midwife, for instance, wrecked telephone kiosks that could cause a fatal delay in calling the emergency services, etc. You should certainly involve POUNC in your battle. Its Chairman is Mr John Morgan who is something of an art connoisseur – he's also Chairman of the British Rail Pension Fund.

The two hundred or so independent Post Office Advisory Committees can also help on a local level. The address should be somewhere in the front of your telephone directory. The committees are usually sponsored by the chamber of trade or local authorities and their representatives do have meetings with local Post Office chiefs and will therefore have the chance to press your case further.

Finally there's the Minister with special responsibility for the Post Office, the Secretary of State for Industry, who is at the Department of Trade and Industry, 1 Victoria Street, London SW1. I just hope your letter gets there.

GIRO

Giro's central computer is in Bootle, on Merseyside, but Giro's Managing Director is not. He prefers to live in London and you can keep in touch with what the computer is up to by writing to him at his office: National Girobank, 10 Milk Street, London EC2V 8JH.

WARD'S LAW: Complain early for Christmas.

PSYCHOLOGY OF COMPLAINING

Many quite legitimate complaints fail because they are badly presented. Here are some of the more common faults:

GRUMBLING: Never let a complaint deteriorate into a moan. Grumblers are a pain in the neck, and if you remind the Area Manager of his nagging wife, he will probably treat you like her.

VERBAL DIARRHOEA: Don't tell the service manager your life history when all you want to report is that a knob has fallen off your telly: 'Well, as I was saying, last night my brother-in-law came round – he's with the army in Germany, you know – and, you know how it is, we had a bit of a celebration like. Then my auntie's friend, Edith, said she likes to watch *Charlie's Angels*. We had a terrible row because Fred – that's my husband – his favourite programme is *The Incredible Hulk* which is on the other channel at the same time. When I finally turned on the telly, the knob came away in my hand. It's under guarantee and I think it's disgusting that . . .'

Come straight to the point. Or by the time you've got to the bit that matters, your listener will be round the corner in the pub downing a badly-needed pint.

THE 'LOOK HERE, MY MAN' APPROACH: This only puts backs up and makes an instant enemy of the one person who is probably in a position to help you. Flatter the man by asking him his *personal* opinion. Don't say, 'This food is off.' Tell him, 'I think if you try this, you will agree that it's off.'

CHANGING HORSES IN MID-STREAM: Don't be side-tracked into complaining about a rude sales assistant when you started out complaining about a non-shrinkable sweater that came out of the wash three sizes too small. Complain about the rudeness, by all means – but only *after* you've sorted out the business of the sweater.

WARD'S LAW: Never show anger without indignation.

PUBLICITY

The most powerful weapons in your armoury are the Press and television.

Companies spend vast sums of money advertising their products and promoting their public image, and they don't like to see a million pounds of goodwill go into the dustbin along with the newspapers.

All in all, there is nothing like the threat of bad publicity for getting British Leyland to take a very personal interest in your new car that's had two new engines, a new gearbox and three new rear axles since you bought it two months ago.

Is everyone afraid of the Press?

Yes. Bus conductors get their backsides kicked by their inspectors when twenty million Sunday newspaper readers are told all about the little Hitler on Route Nine, and small-time sharks lose customers and friends when their unorthodox business methods are exposed by Esther Rantzen.

Will the newspapers be interested in your tale of woe?

Quite likely. Newspapers love stories of bungling bureaucracy, 'Scrooge' gas boards and little old ladies threatened with eviction. If only more little old ladies were evicted, news editors would sleep easily in their beds at night.

The very threat of sneaking to the papers is often enough to shift a few backsides but, if not, you should write to or ring up the news editor of your local newspaper and tell him all about it. He's heard it all before, so the briefer you are, the better your chances of getting a mention.

If you feel you've been particularly hard done by, you

ought to get in touch with one of the popular national news-papers or the news editor of your local TV station. The best time to ring them up is around midday on Sunday, always a quiet news day, when reporters are scratching around for something to put in Monday's paper. The greater your mis-fortune, the happier they will be.

Even if your electric toaster doesn't make the front page, the Press can still help you to win your fight. Many of the popular papers have readers' service columns that will bravely take up your fight for you.

You'll be amazed how a bloody battle with the Gas Board suddenly becomes 'an unfortunate misunderstanding quickly rectified' after a call from a Fleet Street crusader.

WARD'S LAW: Mud sticks where it is thrown.

PUBS

The one really effective way to register a protest against a pub or a brewery is, of course, to give up drinking altogether. I think we can dismiss *that* idea from our minds right away.

Fortunately there are one or two other, less drastic, alternatives open to us. But first a word of explanation about how pubs are run or not run, as the case may be.

There are more than 70,000 pubs in Britain. They can be divided into three groups:

1. *FREE HOUSES. These are one-man-band pubs, owned and run by a landlord who can do exactly what he pleases. He usually does, too. Free Houses account for about a quarter of all our pubs.*
2. *TENANTED HOUSES (about 40,000). These are pubs owned by a brewery but leased to the licensee who usually lives on the premises and runs the place more or less as he likes, so long as he buys the booze from the brewery.*
3. *MANAGED HOUSES (about 15,000). The landlord – or rather manager – is a salaried employee of the brewery and runs it for them.*

Without any doubt the most effective weapon in the drinker's armoury against any pub or its landlord is the boycott.

Canvass as much support as you can among the other regulars and then inform mine host that you will be drinking at The White Swan across the road until you get whatever it is you want. Depending on how many there are of you, and how much serious drinking you do, it shouldn't be long before he sends an emissary across to say he's put the draught lager back on or redecorated the ladies' loo.

This tactic doesn't work if you're only a casual drinker there or just passing through, however. When you have an unhappy experience in a free house, you should speak to the licensee about it. His (or her) name is above the door.

If you don't get anywhere there, that's it I'm afraid. You can jam the fruit machine with bent coins or spill a pint of Guinness on the new carpet, but the best bet is probably to find somewhere more congenial to drink. He won't be sorry and nor will you.

In a tenanted or managed house you have more pull because you can go over the licensee's head and complain to the brewery who, on the whole, don't like to lose customers.

Breweries are in a better position to crack a whip in a managed pub, of course, but if they feel that the churlish behaviour of a tenant is costing them money, it could affect his chances when he wants to renew the lease.

THERE HE GOES—
AND HIS RAPIER LIKE
WIT WITH HIM...

THUD!

The name of the brewery that owns the pub – or the words Free House – is usually hanging outside and you should start off by writing to the Managed Estate Director. As more and more pubs are converted into charmless Formica-topped discotheques, you may well find that the licensee himself is on your side. In which case as many regulars as possible should protest to the Managed Estate Director of the brewery, preferably by letter from a rival pub near by.

The main pub-owning breweries are: Allied Breweries (*Ind Coope, Tetley*, and *Ansells*); Bass Ltd (*Bass, Charrington, Mitchells & Butler, Tennent, Caledonian*); Courage; Scottish and Newcastle; Grand Metropolitan (*Watney, Mann, Truman, Wilsons, Websters, Drybrough, Norwich*); and Whitbread.

The addresses of their head offices can be found in the index at the rear of this book.

All pubs have licences renewable every year at the Brewster Sessions at the local magistrates' court, usually in February. Anyone can object to the renewal of a licence, but flat beer or flat-chested barmaids are not considered sufficient grounds. A disorderly-run house is reason, however, especially if you get the police to support your objection.

WARD'S LAW: Time to complain, gentlemen, please.

THE QUEEN

I think I can say without fear of contradiction that Her Majesty the Queen is not terribly interested in the pop-up action of your electric toaster. She has quite enough trouble getting her own toast to pop up, thank you, and she suggests you do what she does, which is send the wretched thing back to Harrods.

However, the Queen would be very distressed indeed to learn that you, one of her sixty million subjects, were homeless, destitute, or the victim of some appalling injustice due to the incompetence or negligence of one of her Ministers.

How will she ever know of your misfortune?

Well, you could write and tell her. First of all, contrary to popular belief, the Queen often opens the day's mail herself, so there is a good chance she will see your letter. Even when she has been away or busy, she will often ask to see the correspondence that has been dealt with in her absence.

Secondly, as a wife and a mother, the Queen is genuinely sympathetic towards anyone who finds themselves in desperate straits. She won't send you a fiver to see you through to the end of the week; she can't drop by to discuss it over a cuppa, because she's probably busy opening Parliament that day; she doesn't have the time or the resources to send you the kind of thoughtful reply you would get from Marje Proops, either.

But she will pass your letter on to the appropriate

Ministry or organization with a recommendation that they do something about it. And they usually do.

Your letter will be answered not by the Queen herself but by her Private Secretary or Lady-in-Waiting, who will thank you for your letter and advise you what has been done. If nothing is done, then you should write back to the Palace and tell them so. The Queen will not be amused.

Please don't write to the Queen unless you have tried everything else and really are desperate. It would be a terrible shame if our final court of appeal had to stop opening her own letters because the daily mailbag was just too large.

ETIQUETTE NOTE: You should start your letter with 'Your Majesty . . .' (NOT 'Dear Queen . . .') and the envelope should be addressed thus: Her Majesty The Queen, Buckingham Palace, London SW1.

WARD'S LAW: A letter to the Queen can start heads rolling.

RACE DISCRIMINATION

You don't have to be black to be a victim of racial discrimination, but it helps.

If you feel you have been penalized because of your colour – black or white – or because of your 'ethnic origin', then you may have a valid complaint under the Race Relations Act, 1976.

The Act says that any kind of racial discrimination is illegal. Anyone found guilty of discrimination can be fined and ordered to pay you damages – including compensation for hurt feelings.

The Act divides discrimination into two areas:

AT WORK. If your colour or race has prevented you from obtaining a job, or has adversely affected your pay, promotion or prospects, then you can complain to an Industrial Tribunal. What you do is this: write or phone the Race Relations Commission (the address is at the back of this book) and give them all the details of your complaint. They will help you prepare your case for the tribunal and the case will be heard near your home. The court procedure will be exactly the same as for any other employment case heard by the tribunal. (See 'Employers'.)

ALL OTHER DISCRIMINATION. Having difficulty renting a flat? Can't get into the golf club? Laughed at in the pub? Refused credit? If you believe the colour of your skin or your ethnic origin is behind any of these problems, or others like them, then you can take action in the County Court. But, with a bit of luck, things won't have to go that far before you have made your point.

Contact the Commission for Racial Equality, or your local Community Relations Officer (ask at the Town Hall). They will advise you if you have a case and will intercede on your behalf in this distressing matter. They will also tell you how to take the case to court, if it comes to it. The Commission may feel that your case raises such important issues that they will provide a lawyer at their expense to fight for you.

WARD'S LAW: Discriminators go home!

RECEPTIONISTS

Do you know who I feel sorry for? The poor receptionist,
that's who. About ten times a day she's sitting there just
filing her nails when the door bangs open and a customer,
purple with rage, storms in loudly demanding satisfaction.
What a request to make of a lady, indeed!

Give the girl a break. She wasn't there last week. She
won't even be there next week. It wasn't even her fault. She
was filing her nails at the time.

**WARD'S LAW: Save your wrath for the person
who is to blame.**

RED TAPE

The railway clerk demanded a 10p lost-property fee from secretary Sandra Heselden before he would return her lost handbag. Trouble was, all Sandra's money was in the bag. The clerk was adamant: no money, no bag. 'It's the rules,' he said.

So Sandra borrowed 10p from a porter, retrieved her bag, and repaid the porter.

French TV producer Pierre Dugere was rather upset when he wrote off his Lamborghini car on a visit to Britain. He was even more upset when the man from Customs and Excise called on him and told him that as the car had been imported duty-free he still had to pay £2,000 import duty.

Then Mr Dugere had a brilliant idea. He chartered a fishing boat, loaded the wrecked car aboard, and, with a Customs officer as witness, dumped it into the sea over the three-mile limit.

Mr John Millward, paralysed by multiple sclerosis, couldn't obtain the sickness benefit due to him because the Post Office clerk refused to accept his shaky signature on the paying slip.

So Mr Millward's wife Jean forged his signature every week so that her husband was able to collect the benefit due to him.

Mr Peter King arranged for his wife Williamina to collect his income-tax rebate after he left to work in Canada.

But he gave her name as Mrs Peter King – and the taxman said he wasn't authorized to pay out to anyone called Williamina. Nothing could persuade him to pay Williamina her husband's rebate.

So Williamina changed her Christian name to Peter, which she found she could easily do under Scottish law, and collected the money.

American serviceman Andrew Nelson wanted to take his cat Felix home with him to San Francisco, so he asked Trans World Airlines to quote him a price to carry Felix in the baggage compartment.

TWA wanted to know Felix's length 'from tip of nose to base of tail, width across shoulders while in a standing position, and his height from base of paw to top of head (not ears) whilst standing and looking straight ahead'.

Mr Nelson loves Felix, but not that much, so he asked BOAC for a quotation. They told him he could calculate this cost by following these simple rules:

1. Measure the cat's crate in inches and divide the result by 427.
2. Weigh Felix in his crate.

3. The charge is the higher of (1) or (2) above at the appropriate rate, to the minimum charge of £10.40.
4. To this figure add the UK handling charge of £2.75, and the American handling charge, which is about the same.

It was all too much for Mr Nelson. He put Felix in a basket and carried him aboard the plane as hand luggage. Free.

ALL THESE FIVE PEOPLE FOUND THEIR WAY BARRED BY SENSELESS RED TAPE. THEY REALIZED IT WOULD BE FUTILE TO TRY TO CUT THROUGH IT SO THEY GOT WHAT THEY WANTED BY SIMPLY STEPPING UNDER IT AND COMPLAINING LATER.

WARD'S LAW: Don't try to cut red tape. Just step under it.

RESTAURANTS

I have a friend who, whenever he was ordering a meal, used to say to the head waiter: 'I'll pay you if I like it.' He always paid, of course, until one day, after a particularly bad Chinese meal, he announced, 'I didn't like it,' and stood up to leave.

He was chased across Soho by four machete-swinging Chinese waiters and only narrowly escaped becoming the next day's chicken chop suey by dropping a five-pound note.

I mention this because, although my friend didn't know it, he was more or less stating the law on eating out. If the food or service isn't of 'a reasonable standard', you don't HAVE to pay the bill – not all of it, anyway.

What is 'a reasonable standard'?

It all depends on a lot of things – the price, the menu, the kind of restaurant it is, the situation. Obviously something that would be quite acceptable in a Wimpy bar might be intolerable at the Savoy.

This is how the law sees it, anyway: When you order a meal in a restaurant or a café, you are in effect entering a contract with the management – they to supply you with food, you to pay for it.

If they fall down on their side of the bargain and fail to provide the food or the service you might reasonably expect, they are guilty of a breach of contract and you can award yourself 'damages'. This is perfectly legal and is known as 'set off'.

You should certainly refuse to pay the service charge if the waiters are rude and keep you waiting for too long.

MY COMPLIMENTS
TO THE CHEF AND
TELL HIM I'LL MEET
HIM OUTSIDE IN
FIVE MINUTES...

But just how much should be deducted from the rest of the bill depends on how bad things were. In the *Good Food Guide* the Consumers' Association suggests this scale of compensation:

'If you want to make a gesture of disgust, you might say that 10 per cent of the bill would do for your damages for breach of contract. If things were really dreadful make it half. And if they were diabolical, make it 90 per cent.'

At this point it's quite likely that you will have a row. The manager might even call the cops. But as this is a civil and not a criminal matter it has nothing to do with the police and if they don't know it you should tell them so – politely. Providing there was no prior intention on your part to defraud the restaurant, and you have given them your name and address, you have committed no offence by refusing to pay all the bill. The restaurant can always sue you just as you can sue them for damages for pain and suffering if the waiter pours hot soup all over you.

These are your rights in Common Law. Under the Trade Descriptions Act the restaurant also has a duty to live up to its written promises. If 'Fresh Scotch Salmon' on the menu turns out to be frozen Greenland salmon on the plate, the restaurant is guilty of an offence under the Act and can be fined in the magistrates' court.

Similarly, if there is a sign outside saying 'Three-course lunch plus coffee, 40p', they must be able to provide it inside.

Under the Food and Drugs Act, 1955, the restaurant is expected to maintain high standards of hygiene and cleanliness both in and out of the kitchen. The Environmental Health Officer should be told if you have reason to believe the mice aren't fresh.

But as contracts are two-sided agreements, the restaurateur also has a right to expect YOU to carry out certain obligations, too.

When you book a table by phone, for instance, you should turn up on time or at least warn the head waiter by telephone that you are running late. By not turning up at all you are technically guilty of a breach of contract and could be made to compensate the restaurant.

If you find the food or the service disagreeable, you should point it out to the head waiter at the time. He's not psychic, you know. If there's one customer every head waiter hates it's the diner who scoffs the lot, asks for a second helping and then complains about the disgusting food when the bill arrives.

WARD'S LAW: Don't let bossy head waiters bite your head off.

REVENGE

You can be sure of one thing: you're not the first person this has happened to, nor the last. So why not play the Good Citizen occasionally and at least try to prevent your unpleasant experience becoming someone else's.

When you meet inexcusable rudeness or inefficiency, report it to the aggressor's boss. If they were just having an 'off' day, it won't do them any harm. If you're the sixteenth person to complain, they'll be fired, and quite rightly, too.

When you pick a real dead loss out of a hotel or restaurant guide, write to the organization that published it (AA, RAC, Consumers' Association, Egon Ronay or whatever) relating your unhappy experience.

You might just have been unlucky. But if you weren't, you may be instrumental in doing everyone a favour by getting it booted out of the Guide or at least downgraded.

The credit-card people are anxious to know about such places of ill repute who cash in on their good name. You may be too late to get your money back, but you could save someone else a similar fate.

WARD'S LAW: Good complainers fight for the interests of their fellow sufferers.

RUDENESS

Whenever you make yourself a nuisance, someone is bound to be rude to you. A secretary will forget to put her hand over the phone as she says, 'It's that old bag from No. 18 again, Reg.' A dustman will tell you exactly where to put your rubbish.

On top of the frustration and aggravation of whatever it was you were on about, it's the last straw.

It's also the reason why so many complaints fail. Determined to prove that You Won't Be Spoken To Like That, you abandon the original complaint to devote your energies to Teaching the Uncouth Youth A Lesson. Meanwhile, your dustbin still isn't being emptied.

Complain about the rudeness by all means. But don't be sidetracked from getting whatever it was you wanted in the first place.

WARD'S LAW: Don't fight a battle on two fronts at the same time.

SCHOOLS

With the possible exception of health, nothing causes more anxiety and concern than education. Like the Health Service, it's very difficult to know whom to blame when things go wrong, or how to put things right. Like the unpopular patient in hospital, your child could be the one to suffer if you kick up a stink.

If your problem is specifically to do with your child, then the teacher is the first person to see. Talk to other parents who may share your problem. If you're still not getting anywhere, have a quiet word with the Head. Don't adopt the overbearing tone of, well, a head teacher.

If your problem concerns the school as a whole rather than just your own child, then you should seek strength in numbers. Enlist the support of fellow parents and go to the Head. If the problem is outside the Head's authority or you get an unsympathetic hearing, the next step is to start hammering on the door of the local education authority.

The name and address of the Chairman of the Education Committee can be found in the Education Committee's Year Book, a copy of which is in your local library. Education Committee meetings are open to the public, but you can't speak at them.

Put pressure, too, on the paid official who carries out the council's policies, the Chief Education Officer (he may be called the Director of Education).

Education policy is a jungle – a parent can easily get lost or disappear without trace. You soon find out that parents and children apparently have very few rights and their wishes are seldom regarded. You undoubtedly need behind you an organization with clout and experience. Here are a few who will be sympathetic, provide you with ammunition and put you in touch with other parents fighting similar battles.

1. Confederation for the Advancement of State Education (CASE). It has local associations all over the country with a good intelligence system about schools in their district.

2. Advisory Centre for Education (ACE). A sort of Agony Aunt organization that helps State-school parents with their problems. Full of kind words, useful information and helpful suggestions.

3. National Confederation of Parent-Teacher Associations. If your school hasn't got one, they'll tell you how to start and run a PTA.

The addresses of these organizations are in the Index of Addresses at the back of this book.

WARD'S LAW: Don't be a dunce parent.

SERVICING

Here's an entertaining game you can play when you've got nothing better to do. It might save you a lot of money and trouble some day.

Let's say you are thinking of buying a Flood-o-matic washing machine. It certainly *looks* very nice. From all accounts it even *works* quite well. So what you want to know now is: can you get it serviced quickly and cheaply when it goes wrong, as it most certainly will?

You won't get an honest answer from the shop you're planning to buy it from – they're too keen on making a sale to foul their own pitch.

There's only one way to find out: ring up the Flood-o-matic service department and pretend that you are the owner of a sick Flood-o-matic. Ask them how soon they can get an engineer round. Find out how much the standard service charge is. Tell them you fear it needs a new motor. Are the spare parts available without delay?

By the end of the telephone call you will know whether the Flood-o-matic is the machine for you.

Just as few couples go to the altar thinking of divorce, so the last thing that most people consider when they buy something is that it is going to break down.

But whether it is a £7 electric carving knife or a £50,000 Rolls-Royce, it's going to go wrong one day, and the efficiency of the after-sales service network should be a major consideration when you make your choice of product.

Still, this isn't much help to you if you already have a Flood-o-matic that has stopped washing and started flooding . . .

If you call up the shop you bought it from you will almost surely find that the enthusiasm you met when you were buying has mysteriously evaporated. They haven't anyone who can service it. It wasn't a very good model that, anyway, they say . . . but they could give you quite a good trade-in on a new washer.

Thank you and good day, I hope you'll say. But before you hang up, find out from the shop who *will* service it. If they don't know, try the Electricity Board. Failing that, get in touch with the manufacturer.

Most of the most popular domestic appliances in Britain are made by a dozen or so manufacturers, all of whom have service centres dotted about the country.

Some are obliging enough to have their names and addresses in the telephone directory. Others, seemingly under the impression that they are purveyors of washing machines or vacuum cleaners to MI5, seem to keep their whereabouts a trade secret.

Things are made more confusing by the fact that brand names often give no clue to the manufacturer's identity. Is your Flood-o-matic made by the National Electrocution Corporation? Or is it a little-known, now-defunct backwater of Cheat'em Home Industries?

You can find out this information from the Association of Manufacturers of Domestic Electrical Appliances, to which 128 manufacturers belong. They can usually tell you who made your appliance, even if it's foreign, and where the nearest advice centre is.

Having found someone to service your Flood-o-matic, your problems are only just beginning.

There is a peculiar notion entertained by those who work in service departments that they are doing you a favour by condescending to take the back off your vacuum cleaner or whatever. They are not.

Firstly, as you will surely find out when you get the bill, they are being well paid to do the job.

Secondly, until someone can produce an appliance that never goes wrong, every manufacturer has an obligation to the customer to provide an efficient after-sales service with spare parts available for up to ten years after the discontinuation of a particular model.

Failure to do so comes under the heading of unfair trading and should be reported to the Director-General of Fair Trading, Mr Gordon Borrie.

That might get someone into trouble, but it won't unfortunately get your washing machine repaired. The only person who can move mountains there is the Service Director at the manufacturer's head office.

Who is he? Where is he?

Regard it as a challenge to your Sherlock-Holmes-like powers of investigation. For instance, whoever would believe that the Service Director of Morphy Richards is to be found behind a door marked Service Director at the Hotpoint headquarters in Peterborough?

All companies have their equivalent of Service Director and if you're having trouble getting one of their products

fixed, you should knock loudly on their door – when you have found out who and where they are, that is.

Many disputes between customers and service engineers could be avoided if only people bothered to ask for an estimate. But find out beforehand how much the estimate is going to cost. Similarly, a lot of expense could be saved if people sought a second opinion more often.

Engineers are a pessimistic lot on the whole, and they often condemn to death something with years of life left in it – especially if they think they can sell you a new one. A more cheerful chappie round the corner, who hasn't had a row with his wife that morning, might fix it in five minutes. But, of course, if it's not an appliance you can tuck under your arm and take round to the shop, a second opinion may cost you money to save money. It's a gamble that often pays.

If you find yourself in a veritable Japanese wrestling match with a service centre, the Association of Manufacturers of Domestic Electrical Appliances may be able to come to your rescue – provided that the firm carrying out the repair is a member, of course. AMDEA has a consumer complaints department which takes up grievances 'at director level'. If all else fails, there is an arbitration scheme.

You may be as surprised as I was to learn that AMDEA and the Electricity Board have agreed a code of conduct which promises:

1. A service call within three working days.
2. To keep adequate spare parts in stock, even after models have been discontinued.
3. To guarantee rapairs.
4. To complete even the most difficult repair within fifteen days.

In law, a repair must be done in a 'proper and workman-like fashion' and if an electrical appliance has not been repaired to these standards, the firm might have committed an offence. Your local Trading Standards Officer will advise you. In any event, this is a good stick with which to beat the manager of the inefficient and careless service centre.

Many electrical and television shops belong to a trade association called the Radio Electrical and Television Retailers Association (RETRA) which has a similar code of conduct to AMDEA for servicing and repairs carried out by its members. If a member shop lets you down, take it up with RETRA, who have a conciliation scheme.

The statistics of servicing are quite staggering and I mention them merely so you can console yourself with the thought that there are thousands – millions – in the same predicament as yourself.

Forty-one *million* vacuum cleaners, washing machines, food mixers, irons, radios, etc., break down in Britain every year. Even if 99 per cent are fixed properly, that still leaves half a million dissatisfied customers.

Don't let yourself be one of the fuming five hundred thousand *every* time.

I hope this section solves your servicing problem. If it doesn't, let me know and I'll pop back tomorrow and fix it.

WARD'S LAW: Don't let a loose screw give you a nervous breakdown.

SEX DISCRIMINATION

Under the Sex Discrimination Act it is an offence to discriminate against either women or men.

If you're turned down for a job because of your sex, or barred from a pub or refused a mortgage, then you can almost certainly take the offending sexist to court and claim damages for hurt feelings.

The Sex Discrimination Act goes hand in hand with the Equal Pay Act, which makes it illegal to pay a person less than a workmate of the opposite sex doing the same job. It also forbids discriminating against anyone because he or she is married – or unmarried, for that matter.

The two Acts have hardly created the new world that so many women hoped for (and some men feared), but they have gone a long way to changing attitudes and reducing injustice. It's not all stories about male midwives and ladies gatecrashing stag-nights, whatever you read in the newspapers.

How well the new equality laws work depends largely on you and whether you're willing to fight for your rights. So what DO you do if you feel you are being discriminated against?

If you're being discriminated against at work – or while applying for a job – you should take your complaint to an Industrial Tribunal. Don't try to fight this one alone. Involve your union. Write to the National Council for Civil Liberties women's unit. And, of course, you can go to the Equal Opportunities Commission, which was set up to advise you on what to do. It will even pay your legal fees in certain situations. They have also taken up several battles for men who felt they were getting a raw deal – as far as the House of Lords in two cases.

If, on the other hand, you experience discrimination outside your job, this is a case for the County Court. First get in touch with the Equal Opportunities Commission who will try to sort out the problem without a courtroom show-down. If it comes to a punch-up, they'll find you a solicitor experienced in sex warfare. You won't be able to retire on the damages you might receive, but you will have had the satisfaction of having struck a blow for your sex.

WARD'S LAW: Don't let the opposite sex get you down.

SHOPS

John Boyle had a spot of bother with his new washing machine. First the motor had burnt out; then the spin-drier wouldn't work; finally the heater conked out.

The washer was repaired a few times, but just as Mr Boyle thought his troubles were over, it burst into flames, cooking all his smalls and shrinking them to the size of gloves.

The usually patient Mr Boyle took this rather personally. He drove round to the Eastern Electricity Board's showroom in Heathway, Dagenham, positioned the scorched machine outside and stood there beside it with a notice round his neck saying, 'Better things are NOT electric'.

Within two hours, the area manager had called Mr Boyle inside and asked him to choose a new machine.

Don't tell me. You're full of admiration for Mr Boyle but is there some other way of getting what you want without making a ninny of yourself?

Fortunately for us all, there is. It's called the Sale of Goods Act. It puts the retailer – NOT the manufacturer – under a legal obligation to supply goods which are:

1. Of merchantable quality.
2. Fit for the purpose for which they are sold. And
3. Which meet the description applied to them.

It doesn't matter what you are buying – a new car, a packet of hair-clips or a new suit. Nor whether you paid cash or bought it on the HP. Nor whether it was bought in a sale or a discount warehouse or by mail order. Nor whether you bought it two or even five years ago. Providing you can prove that the defect was there when the goods were bought, the law protects you.

What do you do if your new colour telly breaks down a couple of weeks after you bought it then?

Take it back to the place you bought it from and insist that they repair the set free of charge and provide you with another set while they are doing so.

If they refuse, you are legally entitled to get it repaired elsewhere, hire another one in the meantime and recover the cost from the shop that sold you the duff set. Under the Supply of Goods (Implied Terms) Act of 1973, this is your right.

DON'T be fobbed off with suggestions that you should get in touch with the manufacturers – it's up to the shop to sort it out. Your contract is with the *seller*.

The new law is particularly helpful for anyone who has bought a new car. Not only can you hire a replacement every time it has to go back to the garage to be put right, but you can also claim compensation for injury or damage caused by its defects.

Say, for instance, the brakes of your new car failed and you crashed into your house, completely demolishing it.

The garage would then owe you one car and one house.

DON'T take any notice of what the guarantee says, nor of order forms, with small print that says you have to pay the labour charges – thanks to the Supply of Goods (Implied Terms) Act, these statements no longer have any effect in law.

Can you insist on a cash refund?

Yes, if the goods were obviously faulty when you bought them. You don't have to be lumbered with a credit note. And if the shop offers you a replacement you don't have to accept that either. Take no notice of signs which say, 'No cash refunds.'

What happens if the shop digs its heels in?

Take it up at Managing-Director level. If that fails, approach one of the trade organizations to which the shop belongs, to see if they can lean on the shop. Many motor dealers, for instance, are members of the Motor Agents Association, which has an excellent scheme for settling disputes without going to court. Most large stores and shops belong to the Retail Trading Standards Association. Electrical dealers have their Radio, Electrical and Television Retailers Association.

If the product you are complaining about carries a seal of approval of some sort – such as the Woolmark or the British Carpet Centre label – you should get in touch with that body to see what pressures they can bring to bear.

If you still have no success, you'll just have to issue a County Court summons under the Sale of Goods Act. (See 'Suing'.) But usually a persistent and just claim will succeed without you having to go that far.

Can you stop your hire-purchase payments?

Yes – but write telling the hire-purchase company *and* the shop that you are doing so, and why. Under the Supply of Goods (Implied Terms) Act, you are entitled to cease payments if the purchase is clearly not of merchantable quality.

There's additional protection for shoppers who make a purchase with a credit card. If a shop defaults on its obligations (if it goes bankrupt, for instance, leaving you with worthless goods) you can make a claim against the credit-card company under Section 75 of the Consumer Credit Act, 1974.

There are a couple of other battle tactics for dissatisfied customers: If something you buy clearly does not live up to the claims made upon it on the packet or in the advertisements you should ask your local Trading Standards Officer to investigate a possible contravention of the Trade Descriptions Act.

And food that is bad or sold in unhygienic conditions should be referred to your local Environmental Health Officer at the Town Hall for possible prosecution of the shop concerned.

What the law does *not* protect you from is your own mistakes. Contracts are two-sided deals and if you decide, when you get home, that you don't like the colour – that's your bad luck and the shop is under no obligation to refund your money or even give you a credit note.

SHOES

Shoes are the cause of so many complaints that they deserve a special mention. When they fall apart the first day you wear them, the shop assistant blames it all on your hot feet. Or she tells you that they are fashion shoes that were never intended to be worn in the rain. It's a positive incitement to murder.

To avert bloodshed, the shoe industry has agreed a fair-play Code of Practice with the Office of Fair Trading. Most of the big shoe shops are members of the Shoe and Allied Trades Retail Association, and in the event of a dispute, the shoes will be sent off for testing at the Association's Footwear Testing Centre. You have to pay £2 and the shop £4 towards the cost of the tests and the centre's decision is final.

WARD'S LAW: Shop the shop that sells you a pup.

SMALL PRINT

Why is small print so small?

So that you won't bother to read it.

Why don't they want you to read it?

Because, if you did, you would never agree to the conditions.

No one would play a game of cards or football without first finding out what the rules of the game were – especially if the other side wrote the rules.

And yet this is exactly what you do every time you agree to abide by terms and conditions you have never read. Is it surprising that all the goals you score are off-side and that the other side beats you hollow?

Fortunately for us, the small print – or 'exclusion clauses', as they are known – are no longer the bear-traps they used to be. Thanks to the Unfair Contract Terms Act, 1977, no one can wash his hands of responsibility or disclaim liability by pointing to clause *198 (c) iii*, buried away in the terms and conditions.

Those whose coats have disappeared from cloakrooms, whose clothes have been ruined by dry-cleaners, whose cars have been vandalized while in the safe keeping of a car-park attendant, will recognize the new Act as a real boon to the downtrodden customer.

Basically, the Act offers two safeguards.

1. No one can disclaim responsibility for death and injury in any contract or notice. Such signs have no effect in law.

2. Whatever the customer signs or agrees to, liability for

IT'S YOUR OWN FAULT — YOU SHOULD HAVE READ THE SMALL PRINT...

OPTICIAN

BILL

loss or damage cannot unreasonably be avoided. The key word here is 'reasonable'.

To take two extreme examples: Let's say you return to a car park to collect your car, only to find that it has been blown up by armed Arab terrorists who shot dead the attendant on the way out. The car-park management would point to the small print of their terms and conditions stating that they can accept no responsibility for loss of or damage to cars left in their care. It's hardly reasonable to expect car parks to be able to repel armed attackers and it is therefore unlikely that any court would order them to compensate you for the loss of your vehicle. Bad luck, mate, as the judge might say.

But let's suppose that when you returned to collect your car, the attendant was drunk and your car had been stolen. And let's further suppose that this wasn't the first or even the tenth occasion that a car had been spirited away from this thirsty attendant's care. A court would undoubtedly decide that the car-park management had not taken reasonable care of your car and that the 'no responsibility for loss or damage' clause in their terms and conditions was therefore invalid.

The Act interprets negligence as any lack of proper skill

or care. It's a powerful punch which effectively neuters disclaimers that have previously limited your right to claim compensation in just about every situation. Travel agents, builders, cloakroom attendants, dry-cleaners, garages . . . none of these people can duck their responsibilities to the customer any more.

Even the State-owned bully boys, British Rail and the Post Office, can no longer hide behind their punitive terms and conditions which previously gave the customer no rights.

This is not to say you shouldn't read and even take notice of disclaimers. It's no victory, when you're dead, knowing that the sign which said '. . . no responsibility for death or injury' has no effect in law.

If there are terms and conditions which you object to in a contract or agreement, you should still refuse to sign the form or accept the ticket (which commits you to the conditions) until the offending clauses have been removed. It's harder to change the rules once the game is in progress.

WARD'S LAW: Small print, small mind, small heart.

SOD IT

Chairman Mao said: 'Fight no battle you are not sure of winning.' Or, to put it another way: know when to say 'Sod it!'

Life is too short to waste arguing with self-important clerks. You're bigger than that. Just walk away from petty disputes and get on with something more useful, more enjoyable.

By declining to do battle, the victory is yours.

WARD'S LAW: Only fight over 'the principle of the thing' when the thing is worth more money than the time you spend arguing.

SOLICITORS' LETTERS

I have a friend who receives solicitors' letters every week from various firms and people he has upset. The letters threaten all manner of terrible things – impounding his car, taking away his children, seizing his house . . .

He just laughs and chucks them in the wastepaper basket.

In an age when computers sprinkle final final demand notes like confetti, the persistent villain doesn't take such threats very seriously I'm afraid.

He knows how much it's going to cost you to take him to court; he knows that one solicitor's letter will follow another, and another will follow that. He is buying time at your expense – a fiver a letter, perhaps. Solicitors' letters are ten a penny to him – and ten for fifty quid for you.

Save your money. Write it off to experience. Or take out a summons against him right away. Or make his life a misery by employing guerrilla tactics. But don't think you'll bring him to heel with a solicitor's letter.

Are solicitors' letters always so ineffective?

No. Their effectiveness usually increases in direct proportion to the size and reputation of the organization you send them to.

To a large organization with a good name, for instance, being sued by a customer is a considerable embarrassment. It brings unwelcome publicity. It also reflects pretty badly on a management whose customer relations are so bad that you had to threaten to sue them to get anywhere with your complaint.

The same applies to State industries, such as British Rail and Gas and Electricity Boards, where the threat of a law-suit and all the subsequent memo-writing and internal inquests it will provoke is enough to get things moving in your favour.

What is a solicitor's letter and when should you send one?

It is just a very formal way of threatening, 'I'll sue you unless . . .'. The fact that you've gone to the trouble and expense of seeing a solicitor should indicate to the enemy that you're not bluffing and mean business.

You might be threatening to sue a shop for a refund for faulty goods or a travel agent for breach of contract over a holiday.

But whatever the dispute, there's no point in sending a solicitor's letter unless you are legally in the right – because you can be pretty sure that the enemy's solicitor will read the letter and your bluff will be called.

How can you send a solicitor's letter and how much does it cost?

If you don't have a solicitor, your Citizens' Advice Bureau or local Law Society will recommend one. Tell them briefly what your battle is about because solicitors specialize and it helps if you can get an expert in that particular field.

You might find a solicitor to write a letter for £5, but I doubt it. Ten pounds is nearer the mark, depending on how complicated your problem is, and it could end up costing you much, much more. You are, after all, paying for his knowledge and legal experience as well as his time.

BUT . . . depending on your circumstances, you might be entitled to free legal advice.

There's a scheme called 'the green form scheme', designed to give badly-off people £25 of free legal advice and assistance, and covers everything from making a will to taking on your landlord. Less badly-off people have to make a contribution under this scheme.

There's also Legal Aid. You have to earn less than £2,400 a year to qualify for it – but ask for details at your local Citizens' Advice Bureau, anyway.

Finally, if you are fortunate enough to have a Law Centre or a Legal Advice Centre in your neighbourhood, you will be able to obtain free advice from a solicitor, who will almost certainly fire off a letter on your behalf. But don't expect something for nothing if you turn up in a Rolls-Royce.

WARD'S LAW: Never send a solicitor's letter unless you intend to follow it all the way to court.

SUBTERFUGE

Nobody ever won a dogfight by playing fair. When honest methods fail you must lie, cheat and bluff your way to victory.

Whenever you come up against a brick wall, just answer the question, 'How would James Bond get round this one?' The solution is surprisingly simple if only you use a bit of cunning.

THE WALK-STRAIGHT-IN TACTIC

If you can't get an appointment to see someone who is avoiding you, walk uninvited into his office. It doesn't matter how big the office block is. No commissionaire will stop you if you walk briskly and business-like with a folder under your arm.

Make for the lifts and go up to the third floor. Ask someone there what floor your target is on. Say his secretary is waiting for you by the lift but she forgot to say which floor to come to.

Another walking-in technique is to ring up your target's firm beforehand and ask to speak to the postal department or main reception. Say you are Interflora and could you have Mr So-and-So's correct room number so that an order you are about to send doesn't go astray. If it's room 416 the chances are it will be room 16 on the fourth floor.

THE PUT-ME-THROUGH-IT'S-URGENT PLOY

You'd think some managing directors were Howard Hughes the way they hermetically seal themselves off from the outside world. They will break their self-imposed vow of silence to discuss only one thing: money.

Call his secretary and say you have found a banker's draft for £1,186 made out to the company. Say that you refuse to discuss the return of it with anyone except the Managing Director. If she stalls say that if that's all a thousand pounds means to her company, you'll save yourself the trouble and chuck it away.

She will then put you through to the Managing Director.

CHECK THEIR STORY OUT

Don't believe everything you're told. If a service manager says he can't get on with your repair because the manufacturer or agent doesn't have a certain spare part in stock,

ring up and ask them yourself. Or pretend to be from the firm's stores and find out whether or not the part has ever been ordered. Armed with this information, you can go back and create hell.

WARD'S LAW: Embarrass your way to victory by catching the enemy with his trousers down.

SUING

Some battles can't unfortunately be won by charm, threats, persistence, string-pulling or reasoned pleas. When you come up against a brick wall, you have to decide whether to back down and forget the whole thing, or to go to court to get justice.

It's at this point most people give up. Court cases have the reputation of being ruinously expensive – with absolutely no guarantee, of course, that the baddie won't win. Don't you believe it.

Civil disputes involving claims of more than £2,000 have to be settled in the High Court. With that amount of money at stake you really ought to have a solicitor, and if you don't have one, the Citizens' Advice Bureau or your local Law Society will put you in touch with one. They will also advise you if you are eligible for legal aid.

But most disputes are over smaller amounts than this – maybe £10 or £20 for a pair of shoes – and these are dealt with by the County Court. They are known as 'small claims'.

All disputes involving less than £200 are considered to be small claims and they are heard privately by the County Court Registrar rather than in open court. The two sides can still produce evidence and call witnesses, of course, but there's absolutely no need to have a solicitor representing you. The atmosphere is informal and, best of all, whether you win or lose the costs are minimal and neither side can claim legal expenses against the other.

The procedure for making a small claim – or for defending one – is exactly the same as a larger action. (I explain later in this chapter the formalities that have to be followed, giving two examples of suing and being sued.)

It cannot be stressed often enough that County Court cases needn't be expensive. You don't have to have a solicitor to win. You just have to be confident that (a) you are legally in the right and (b) that you have the determination to see the case through.

There are two ways of taking your fight to court.

1. Sue the villain.
2. Let the villain sue you.

If you can possibly arrange things so that you're the one who is sued, it makes things a whole lot easier.

Why? Well, obviously if you have already parted with your money and the villain refuses to compensate you for the faulty goods, or the results of his negligence, bad workmanship, or whatever, you're the one who has to prise open his mean little palm to get your cash back.

But if by good fortune you haven't actually paid him yet, the boot's on the other foot. He's the one who has to sue for his ill-deserved money.

Since nine out of ten County Court cases are brought by firms against customers, we'll start there.

BEING SUED

Let's say you have had some alterations done to your house. The bill comes to £590, but a week after the builders move out, the plaster cracks and faulty plumbing causes a pipe burst which ruins a carpet.

The builders deny responsibility, so you knock three hundred quid off their bill to cover the damage – and send them a cheque for £290. (It's important that you should pay them something for the work they have done, because if it does get to court, you then have some proof of your reasonableness.)

After a lot of angry words, they sue you for the £300 they claim you still owe them, denying that they are in any way responsible for the mini-disaster.

What happens when you are sued?

You receive a summons, which is simply a piece of paper stating who is suing you, for how much, for what and when and where.

Some people ignore summonses, hoping that they will go away. They are amazed when, two months later, they learn that the case was heard in their absence and that they have to fork up not only the money they are being sued for, but also the legal costs of the other side.

Others are so overwhelmed by the prospect of the expense and trauma of going to court, they immediately settle up, even though they believe they're in the right.

But you're made of stronger stuff than that, I hope.

Providing your dispute is a reasonably straightforward one, you can probably manage quite nicely without a solicitor.

There's quite a lot of bureaucratic form-filling involved, but it's not much worse than applying for a driving licence. The Clerk of the Court can't give you legal advice, but he will guide you through the jungle of legal terminology and help you fill in the forms correctly.

Indicate on the papers sent to you by the court that you will be defending the case, giving the brief details of what your defence is. This must be returned to the court within fourteen days.

With any luck the enemy will withdraw their case as soon as they know you intend to fight it. A summons is more often a try-on than a serious intent to sue you and, incredibly, *70 per cent* of cases brought by firms against customers are withdrawn as soon as a defence is filed.

If they're not bluffing, however, you now have to:

1. Decide whether you are going to fight it yourself without the help of a solicitor. Or
2. Get a solicitor.

In civil actions, Legal Aid is available only if the claim exceeds £200 – and if you're pretty poor. You can find out whether or not you are entitled to Legal Aid from the Clerk of the Court or from your local Citizens' Advice Bureau.

But if, like most of us, you are medium broke and medium bright, you can almost certainly go it alone if you have a strong case.

But before you do anything, you should rush out and invest £2.50 in an excellent Consumers' Association book called *How to Sue in the County Court*. It not only tells you what to do, blow by blow, but with a bit of practice in front of the mirror turns you into a veritable Perry Mason. When you win your case, you may well decide to give up your job on the buses for something more lucrative at the Bar.

If you can't find a copy of *How to Sue* in a bookshop, you can get it 25p cheaper by mail order from the Consumers' Association at: Caxton Hill, Hertford. There's another excellent paperback – free – called *Small Claims in the County Court*, published by the Lord Chancellor's office, who will send you one. It's also available at County Courts. You'll find it a great little pocket attorney.

If, even after sitting up all night learning how to become a do-it-yourself lawyer, you feel that you could do with a chat with a legal eagle, you can do so without it costing a fortune, and possibly even for free. In fact, you'd be mad *not* to seek advice. This is how to set about it. You can:

1. Have a chat with the legal expert at your Citizens' Advice Bureau.

2. Visit (if you have one) your neighbourhood Legal Advice Centre or Law Centre.

3. Make use of the 'green form scheme'. This is a scheme

*for badly-off people and it provides free legal advice costing up
to £25, depending on your circumstances. Again, ask for details
at your Citizen's Advice Bureau.*

*4. Fixed Fee Interview Scheme. For £5, whatever your
means, you get a thirty-minute consultation with a solicitor in
the Legal Aid system. Your local CAB will put you in touch
with one.*

Defending yourself in court isn't nearly as frightening
or as complicated as it sounds. If the case is due to be heard
many miles away, you can write to the Registrar requesting
that it is transferred to a court nearer your home because of
the hardship that travelling would cause you.

You can also ask for the case to go to arbitration, which
is a more informal, less expensive – but equally binding –
way of settling the dispute round a table. But the other side
has to agree to it. (All small claims of £200 or less go to
arbitration automatically.)

Either way, before the case is heard, there is a 'pre-trial
review' at which both sides get together with the registrar
of the court to try to hammer out a last-minute settlement.
You should take along to this meeting all your evidence –
bills, receipts, letters, etc. Very often a compromise peace
solution can be worked out without the full panoply of
the law.

Failing that, you will just have to fight it out in court.

Don't be intimidated by the fact that the other side has
solicitors and barristers – it won't count against you. On the
contrary, it will probably make the judge listen even more
sympathetically to your plight.

HOW TO SUE

Before you even begin, three don'ts:

DON'T sue just because you are angry with someone,
however tempted you are to smash them into the ground. It
might be six months before the case comes to court by which

time your anger – and with it your determination – will have subsided considerably.

DON'T sue until you are absolutely certain that you have a good claim in law. You may have been treated unfairly – but your legal rights have to be violated if you are going to win.

DON'T sue someone who hasn't any money. It's paper money you're after, not a paper victory.

Right, then. Ready to do battle?

Let's take the dispute with the incompetent builder again (there are a lot of them around, after all), only this time we'll assume that you have already paid the full £590 and are now trying to recover £300 for the damage caused by his negligence.

This is what you do:

1. Write to him, by recorded delivery, saying that unless he coughs up within seven days you will sue him for breach of contract and negligence. He either ignores your letter altogether, or rebuffs you. Your next step is:

2. Look up the address of the nearest County Court in the telephone directory under 'Courts' and go along there. Tell the Clerk you wish to take out a summons.

He will help you fill out a 'Request Form' to set the case going, and will advise you on what sort of summons you ought to take out. (A 'default summons' is to recover a fixed sum of money; an 'ordinary summons' is to recover unspecified damages.) You can then fill out a 'Particulars of Claim' form, giving all the facts.

Don't be put off by all the legal jargon and don't hesitate to ask the Clerk to translate or explain anything you're not sure about. He's not allowed to become your legal adviser, even if he wanted to be, but he will steer you in the right direction.

When you have finished filling in all the paperwork, the court issues the summons for you. What could be easier? Well, a lot of things, actually, but don't be put off.

It's important to get the name and address of the person or firm you are suing correct, by the way. If it is a non-Limited Company you are suing, you must know not only the proper name of the company, but also the address at which it carries on business.

If the firm is a Limited Company, the summons has to be sent to the company's registered office, which may not be the address you're familiar with. This information, if all else fails, is available at the Companies Registration Office at Companies House in London. You can call in personally and make a search, or write to or phone Companies House and ask them to recommend a search 'agency', who will make the search for you for a modest fee of about £5.

How much is all this going to cost you?

Not very much, really. For claims not exceeding £150, you have to pay a court fee of only £1.50, which rises to a maximum of £19 for claims of £2,000.

What deters many people from going to law, of course, is the thought of having to pay the other side's legal expenses. But if you are suing someone for less than £200 – say a shop over a pair of shoes that fell to pieces – then the other side can't claim its legal costs from you, even if you lose.

For claims up to £1,000, the most you are liable to pay the other side in costs is limited to £9. Up to £2,000, the maximum is £13. In effect, your day in court could cost you less than the price of dinner for two in the West End.

Your case probably won't get to court, anyway.

A mud-slinging, time-consuming court case is far more damaging to a firm than to you, since it is bound to suffer from the bad publicity the case will attract. You will most probably find that you are offered an out-of-court settlement as soon as your summons is served on the enemy.

WARD'S LAW: A good settlement is better than a bad victory.

SWEARING

Under Section 28 of the Town Police Clauses Act (1847) it is an offence punishable by a fine of £20 (or fourteen days), to tell someone to **** off! Or to go and **** themselves.

But more serious than the risk of putting yourself in the clink is the fact that by swearing you put yourself firmly in the wrong.

The same goes for that much-loved sign-language equivalent, the V-sign. Even when used between hostile motorists, the police can take the view that a V-sign was tantamount to 'behaviour likely to cause a breach of the peace'.

As a professional complainer you should have an adequate vocabulary of abuse without having to resort to loutish insults. Practise a little invective in front of the mirror before going to bed at night. After all, karate requires hundreds of hours of practising before you are capable of delivering a death blow.

Far from cramping your style, the laws on swearing can actually be made to work *for you*. Next time someone calls you a ****ing ****, you might feel inclined to make an official complaint to a policeman or to press charges at the local police station. You don't have to have a witness, though the more supporting evidence you can offer, the stronger your chances of victory.

You could also take a private summons by swearing an information before a magistrate (the Clerk at the magistrates' court would help you do this). But if you lost the case you might have to pay the costs of the **** you accused.

WARD'S LAW: He who swears is lost.

SWITCHBOARDS AND SECRETARIES

The switchboard operator is probably the only person in the entire organization who knows who everyone is and where to find them. Can you say the same for the Managing Director?

And yet, in spite of the key front-line jobs switchboard operators hold, many callers talk to them as if they were fully automated dialling devices instead of people.

Talk to a switchboard operator like a robot and she (or he) will handle your call like one and you'll spend the rest of the day being transferred from extension to extension or 'holding'.

Talk to her like a human being and you'll get preferential human treatment.

Make the switchboard operator your friend. As briefly as possible explain your problem and ask her advice. She can tell you the name of the person you ought to talk to and, if he's not there, when is the best time to contact him. She might even know where he's having lunch.

SECRETARIES

After trial by switchboard operator comes trial by secretary.

Far more important than winning the sympathy or attention of the Managing Director is getting his secretary on your side. He may give the orders, but she's the one who gets things done. She's also the one he turns to for advice.

If she likes you, your telephone calls will be put through, your letters will be at the top of the tray when he arrives in the morning, and she'll jog his memory for you if he forgets to do something. You will have someone rooting for you in the heart of the enemy's command tent!

Fall out with her and you're on a loser right from the start. Your letters and telephone calls will be held back from him because 'he's terribly tied up just now'. When he asks her what's been happening she'll undermine your credibility by saying, 'Nothing important. That neurotic Anderson woman called three times, but I managed to put her off.'

How can you win over a secretary?

By being a bit of a creep, that's how. By talking to her as if she's not just a typist, for a start. Find out her name from the switchboard in advance so that you can say when she answers the phone, 'Is that Miss Wright?' as if you've heard all about her. Involve her in your problem instead of leapfrogging over her like everyone else does.

Be a bit conspiratorial, even. 'I know he's got a lot on his plate, but if you could shove my letter under his nose again when he's got a moment, I'd be very grateful. May I call you in an hour about it?' Don't sound grovelling, though.

Charm and flatter her, but never patronize or talk down to her.

What if she's a cow?

It does happen, of course. Some over-protective secretaries see their role not so much as a filter, more an impenetrable fortress. If you are fairly certain your letters *aren't* getting through to him, then try marking them Private and Confidential. Only real dragons open private mail.

If that fails then find out his home address (see 'Aggro') and apologize for invading his privacy, explaining why you had no choice. It could be he has no idea what the dragon is like.

WARD'S LAW: Make friends to influence people in the enemy's camp.

TAX INSPECTORS

Question Number One: Would you engage in conversation a non-English-speaking Swahili nuclear physicist on the subject of thermodynamics?

Question Number Two: So what makes you feel you are qualified to discuss your financial affairs with one of HM's Inspectors of Taxes?

Disputes between ordinary mortals and those civil servants employed to fill the nation's purses are best left to those who speak the language and understand the game: accountants.

Can you afford an accountant?

Can you afford NOT to have an accountant is more to the point. Civil servants are not paid to volunteer information (they're too busy, anyway). If your shirt-tail is hanging out or you are owed £150 tax rebate due to the demise of your great-aunt, it won't be HM Inspector who points it out. Most accountants, on the other hand, consider it a personal challenge to deprive the Exchequer of as much money as possible in order to ingratiate themselves with their clients.

Where do you find an accountant?

In the same place that you find pest-control experts and scrap-yard merchants: the Yellow Pages directory. There are pages and pages of accountants, so pick one with the same name as yourself, for no better reason than that he can't forget it.

Accountants charge for the amount of work they do, so the simpler you make it for them – feeding them with all the necessary accounts and receipts, etc. – the less you will pay. ALWAYS REPLY TO LETTERS FROM THE INLAND REVENUE. Silence is suspicious – and costly.

The Inland Revenue considers you guilty until you have proved yourself innocent. If you receive an assessment and chuck it away, you will end up having to pay up *even if you don't owe them the money*.

Tax inspectors like to receive replies to their letters. It makes them feel wanted. Write them a letter saying simply: '*I hereby give you formal notice of appeal against the assessment for 1974–5 on the grounds that it is estimated and excessive.*'

Those few words buy you more time – maybe months – and enable you or your accountant to appeal to the General Commissioners. But find yourself an accountant before wandering into that financial forest.

What should you do if the Inland Revenue keep on pestering you for money you don't owe – like sending you tax demands for the present earnings of your late husband who died five years ago?

It depends on how much of a sense of humour you have about it. You could write a simple letter pointing out the facts, get a dozen copies made, and send one off as each new demand comes in.

But if you feel you have suffered an appalling injustice under the tax man – by being unjustly hounded, or by being unable to recover money owed to you – you should ask the Ombudsman, Mr Cecil Montacute Clothier, QC, to intercede on your behalf.

Mr Clothier – his more fancy title is the Parliamentary Commissioner for Administration – has struck many fine blows for the downtrodden taxpayer, winning refunds and apologies and, at the same time, booting autocratic official-dom up the backside.

He can't be approached by you directly, unfortunately, but he will investigate any case brought to him by an MP. So you must first write to your MP.

WARD'S LAW: Pay nothing in tax today that you can argue about tomorrow.

TAXIS

The London taxi driver is not a happy man.

His passengers cause him a lot of aggravation and then don't tip him properly. The police persecute him under laws drafted in the days when taxis were horse-drawn hansom carriages. And mini-cab drivers deprive him of his living.

Add to this the fumes and frustration of driving in London traffic all day and you have a man who would happily strangle – well, you.

Before we discuss ways of antagonizing him still further, a few words about what the driver of a black cab in London must do for you under the Hackney Carriage Act.

Does he have to take you?

There is a popular myth that a taxi driver has to stop when he sees you standing on the street corner frantically waving your arms. If only it were true! He does not have to. He can drive around London all day with his For Hire sign on if he likes and not stop for anyone. Nor does he have to take you if you jump into his empty cab when he stops at traffic lights.

The only time he is obliged to accept a fare is:

1. If he is standing at an authorized taxi-rank. And

2. If he pulls into the kerb in response to your signal and 'parleys' with you, as the law puts it – and only then if your journey is not more than six miles or one hour in duration *and providing it starts and ends within the Metropolitan Police District.*

DOES HE HAVE TO SET HIS METER?

Yes, always. And, providing that a journey begins and ends in the Metropolitan Police area, you have to pay only what is on the meter.

CAN A DRIVER EVER BARGAIN OVER A FARE?

Only if your destination is outside the Metropolitan Police District. Providing you do not leave the District, you pay only what is on the meter.

WHAT ABOUT THE AIRPORT?

There are a slightly different set of rules for Heathrow Airport, because there were complaints of highway robbery by taxi drivers almost every day. A taxi driver doesn't have to take you to the airport, but if he accepts the fare, he has to set the meter *and that is what you pay*.

At the airport a driver is obliged to set his meter for journeys up to twenty miles that end in the Metropolitan Police District and, again, you pay only what is on the meter.

He is, however, allowed to negotiate fares that take him away from London – even if it's only a couple of miles in the other direction.

IF A DRIVER CONTRAVENES ANY OF THESE REGULATIONS HE CAN BE SUMMONSED UNDER THE HACKNEY CARRIAGE ACT AND BE BROUGHT BEFORE A MAGISTRATE.

A summons has to be issued within five days of the offence being committed, so it has to be reported straight away if you are to get the driver to court.

You can report the offence at any police station, but it is probably better to inform the police department responsible for enforcing the taxi laws – the Metropolitan Police Public Carriage Office at 15 Penton Street, London N1. Call in there, or write to the Senior Executive Officer, giving details of how you were wronged.

You have to be able to identify the cab driver, of course. This shouldn't be too difficult since he and his cab have three identifying serial numbers through which he can be traced.

1. The registration number of the cab, at the front and rear, just as every vehicle has.

2. The 'plate number' of the taxi. When a cab is licensed by the police it is given a five-figure number which has to be displayed on the boot at the back of the cab and inside the passenger compartment.

3. The driver's badge number which he is supposed to wear or display on duty. This is the one to get if you can, since it is *his* number. The taxi, on the other hand, might be driven by several cabbies and the police will have to find out which one.

WHAT IF THE DRIVER IS JUST PLAIN RUDE OR DELIBERATELY TAKES A LONG WAY ROUND?

You can still complain to the Public Carriage Office which has the power to revoke or withdraw a driver's licence to ply for hire.

Let's take an everyday occurrence. Say you give a 5p tip to a driver on a 50p fare. For several seconds he stares unbelievingly at this small coin in his palm and then flings it across the road.

If you lodged a complaint, he would be called into the Carriage Office, told of the accusation and asked for an explanation. He would then be reminded that passengers are not obliged to pay any more than is due on the clock, and warned that if it happens again they won't take such a lenient view. (They will, of course, but if it happens a third time he might be in serious danger of losing his licence when it comes up for renewal after three years.)

Accusations that a driver has taken his passenger on a trip around the houses are rather more tricky. A driver isn't obliged to take the shortest route – he can go any way he decides is quickest according to the road and traffic situation.

What happens is this: the journey is retraced on a map and if he was obviously trying to pull a fast one, he'll get clobbered.

The Public Carriage Office, incidentally, is also the place where all property lost in London taxis gets taken – if you're lucky, of course. You pay a percentage of the value to the driver as a reward.

TAXIS OUTSIDE LONDON: All taxis – that is, licensed cars with meters – have to be registered either with the police or the local council. It varies from town to town, but a call to the police will tell you who cracks the whip.

MINI-CABS: Mini-cab drivers answer to no man, which is largely why they are so detested by licensed cab drivers. A mini-cab driver has to pass no tests on his knowledge of a city, nor for that matter does the car he drives.

Prevention is therefore wise and more certain than a cure. Only travel in mini-cabs that work for established mini-cab firms. That way, if something goes wrong, you can complain to the control. Find out how much a journey is going to cost you before you start. It saves arguments the other end when you are charged twice what you expected.

WARD'S LAW: Don't let your taxi-driver take you for a ride.

TV AND RADIO

How often do you turn off the television or the radio at the end of a programme and exclaim, 'What a load of rubbish *that* was!'?

Well, instead of telling your family, why not tell the people who put on the rubbish exactly what you thought about it? After all, if they don't hear from you, they might think you liked it.

Hold a one-man phone-in protest to the TV or broadcasting studios. It only costs 3p to phone and it will make you feel a whole lot better about wasting all that valuable time in front of the box.

Here's what to do. Ring up the TV company that put out the programme and ask to speak to the Duty Officer. Ask him to log your complaint and your remarks about the programme. Be polite, though – he wasn't the producer, you know.

If you feel strongly enough about it, follow it up next day with a letter to the Programmes Controller, or in the case of BBC Radio, the Managing Director.

If it was an ITV programme, you could hammer another nail home by writing to the Complaints Review Board of the Independent Broadcasting Authority.

Here are your phone-in protest numbers. Keep them by your set:

BBC TV	London 01-743 8000
BBC Radio	London 01-580 4468
Thames TV	London 01-387 9494
London Weekend	London 01-261 3434

ATV	London 01-262 8040
	Birmingham 021-643 9898
Border	Carlisle 0228-25101
Grampian	Aberdeen 0224-53553
Westward	Plymouth 0752-69311
HTV	Cardiff 0222-26633
Scottish	Glasgow 041-332 9999
Channel	Jersey 0534 23451
Granada	Manchester 061-832 7211
Southern	Southampton 0703-28582
Yorkshire	Leeds 0532-38283
Anglia	Norwich 0603-28366
Tyne-Tees	Newcastle-upon-Tyne 0632-610181
Ulster	Belfast 0232-28122

Bad or boring programmes are one thing, but when you yourself have been unfairly treated on the radio or on television, you may want to do more than give someone an earful.

The BBC has a Programmes Complaints Commission, an independent committee which investigates allegations of 'unwarranted invasion of privacy and misrepresentation'.

You must complain in writing within thirty days of the programme and, if your complaint is upheld, the guilty Beeb men are suitably reprimanded. One snag is that you can't complain to the Commission and then sue the BBC for libel – they make you sign an undertaking waiving all rights of legal redress. But, as with the Press Council, there's nothing to stop you suing and then complaining later.

WARD'S LAW: Take a dim view of a dim view.

THOSE ARE THE RULES

There is no arguing with the man or woman who folds his arms and says with that air of utter finality, 'Those are the rules, I'm afraid.'

They didn't make the rules, as they will surely tell you two or three times, but, by God, they're going to stick to them.

What you have to do is find a way around those rules. You'll be surprised how many loopholes you can find when you put your mind to it. The more idiotic the rule, the more idiotic the person who drew it up – and the more holes there are in it.

EXAMPLE: You are in a hurry to go away on holiday and you have arranged for a friend to collect the keys to your flat from the caretaker. But the caretaker says, 'I'm sorry, but I am not allowed to accept the responsibility of keys. It's more than my life's worth.'

He is however permitted to take in letters.

SOLUTION: Put the keys in an envelope and don't tell him what it contains.

I won a great victory against a British Rail guard who saw me boarding a train a few years ago carrying a four-feet high mirror under my arm.

'I suppose you've got a ticket for that,' said the guard.

'But this is luggage, surely?' I protested.

'Luggage?' said the guard, as if I were demented. 'That's not luggage. That's goods, and as far as the Railway is concerned you have to have a child's ticket for it.'

I knew immediately I was speaking to a man deaf to

reason. A quick flick through the BR Book of Rules and Regulations at the information office saved me paying £3.00 child's fare for my mirror, however.

I wrapped the mirror in newspaper, ran a strip of tape round it – and changed its status from child to 'accompanied luggage'. Cost: one copy of *The Times*, one roll of sticky tape.

WARD'S LAW: Rules are made to be got round.

TRADE DESCRIPTIONS ACT

We all get conned once in a while. As a matter of fact, we all get conned twice in a while.

The Trade Descriptions Act doesn't always get our money back, but it does give us the satisfaction of seeing the smooth-talking con-man (or con-organization) fined up to £400 or jailed for two years.

This is how it works . . .

It is against the law to sell anything in Britain by pretending it is something it isn't. For instance, an offence has been committed:

IF you buy a 'mink' coat that turns out to be a genuine rabbit.

IF you buy a second-hand car with 5,000 miles on the clock and you later find out it has done 25,000 miles.

IF the holiday brochure promises you a luxury hotel with a bathroom and a view of the sea and you end up in a no-star hotel overlooking Benidorm railway station.

IF the ninety-minute cleaner takes four days to dry-clean your best tie.

IF you go to see a sex film that's advertised as wicked and depraved and it turns out to be a rather prudish re-hash of *Mary Poppins*.

This misleading description doesn't even have to be in writing. If a used-car salesman verbally assures you a car is 'in mint condition', and a week later the rusted bottom falls out, you've got him by the short and curlies.

WHAT DO YOU DO IF YOU FEEL YOU'VE BEEN CHEATED?

Go and see the Trading Standards Officer in charge of the area where you and your money were parted from each other (i.e., if you booked your dud holiday with a tour operator in Bond Street, the Westminster Trading Standards Officer is the man to see). The address is in the phone book under the name of the council. (Some Trading Standards Officers are still called Weights and Measures inspectors, but their job remains the same.)

Tell him exactly how you wuz robbed. If he thinks an offence was committed, he will institute proceedings and you will probably have to give evidence in the magistrates' court.

THAT'S ALL VERY WELL, BUT WHAT ABOUT GETTING YOUR MONEY BACK?

Since the introduction of the Criminal Justice Act, 1972, offenders under the Trade Descriptions Act are often ordered to pay compensation to their victims. But if no order is made, you can still bring an action in the civil courts under the Sale of Goods Act – though it is unlikely any firm would let it go that far.

WARD'S LAW: Make the law work for you.

TRAFFIC WARDENS

The traffic warden knows exactly why your car is parked where it shouldn't be. You were just nipping into the tobacconist to buy some cigarettes? No?

Then you were unloading this incredibly heavy consignment of . . . No?

In which case you must have been collecting an urgent prescription for your sick mother. Yes, of course . . .

If wardens had a pound for every cast-iron excuse they were given by errant motorists, they would soon be millionaires. Unfortunately they are paid to issue parking tickets, and you can hardly blame them if once in a while they stick one to your windscreen.

Look what happens when they don't. Mrs Elsie Tallents, 41, a traffic warden in Manchester, used to book only one motorist some weeks. 'If the cars were not there to book, it was not my fault,' she said.

Mrs Tallents was fired.

Although motorists spend a great deal of time moaning about wardens, it's surprising how little they know about either wardens or the tickets they issue.

WARDENS are an auxiliary of the police force and come under the Chief Constable (or, in London, the Metropolitan Police Commissioner). They are responsible for enforcing the parking regulations and are supposed to issue a ticket for every offence they see committed.

Some, out of the kindness of their hearts, allow us a few minutes' grace, but once the first stroke of the pen has been

made, they are obliged by law to complete the ticket and issue it.

After a ticket has been issued, a copy goes to a central ticket office manned by a civilian police staff whose job it is to find out the name of the driver and to make sure he coughs up the cash. The central ticket office has nothing to do with the wardens.

PARKING TICKETS are not fines, as most people think. The £6 white ticket is a fixed 'penalty' that in effect allows you to buy your way out of being prosecuted for a parking offence. You may if you wish go to court instead, but unless you're legally in the right and can prove it, I wouldn't, if I were you, because you'll end up being found guilty and fined twice that amount.

The £2 or £4 yellow tickets issued when you overstay your welcome on a meter by not more than half an hour, are exactly what they say – 'an excess charge'. You haven't committed any offence – you simply chose to stay on for that extra time at a vastly more expensive rate payable to the local council. (It is an offence not to pay the excess, however, and if you stay on any longer, you also collect a white £6 ticket.)

What can you do if you feel you have been booked unfairly?

If your car is parked where no parking is allowed, then – unless your vehicle has broken down – you are guilty of an offence.

(Running out of petrol is no excuse, by the way, since the law takes the view that this was caused by 'insufficient preparation'.)

But the Great Parking Warden In The Sky is merciful and tickets are sometimes cancelled if there are 'mitigating circumstances'.

You have to be able to prove it, however. With a garage receipt that confirms you did break down where and when you said you did. Or a doctor's note saying that you were collecting an urgent prescription.

Write to the Officer in Charge at the ticket office, the address of which is on the white £6 ticket (in London it's Miss B. Arnold, 39 Portman Square, W1H 9FH). Remember they're no fools and your excuse is quite likely to be looked into by an 'investigative unit' attached to all ticket offices.

It helps your case if you managed to catch the traffic warden actually making out the ticket, because you can ask him (or her) to make a note of your excuse of the day on the back of the ticket.

What if you complain about the warden and not the ticket?

Well, you can always do what a Birmingham motorist did. He knocked the meter maid's hat off and jumped up and down on it for several minutes. He was fined £25 for assault and ordered to buy her a new hat. He said it was worth every penny.

But it might be more advisable to write to the Chief Constable (or Police Commissioner in London) who will pass on your complaint to Big Chief Meter Man.

DON'T, incidentally, make the mistake of confusing a yellow-band traffic warden ('mustard man' or 'meter maid' as they are popularly known) for a common-or-garden meter *attendant*, who has a blue ribbon round his (or her) hat. A meter attendant is employed by the local council only to check cars on meters, and has no authority to issue tickets to cars parked on yellow lines.

In this country it is no crime for people to be happy in their work, so if a meter maid happens to be smiling or singing , 'Oh, What a Beautiful Morning . . .' as she slaps a ticket on your windscreen, you have no grounds for complaint.

WARD'S LAW: Don't blame traffic wardens for doing their job.

TREES

Only one thing came between postman Andie Boggie's house and an uninterrupted view of a nearby power station: a very beautiful 300-year-old elm tree.

It was with some dismay, therefore, that one morning Mr Boggie observed two workmen bearing saws and axes, arrive at the foot of the 70ft-high tree.

Mr Boggie realized that unless he did something pretty quickly, he would soon be looking out on a power station instead of a leafy elm.

What did he do? He climbed up the tree on the Devon Park Estate at Newark, Notts – and refused to come down until the tree was reprieved. After all, he reasoned, you can't chop a tree down while there's a postman up it, can you?

Nine hours later, at an emergency meeting of the local parks committee, a stay of execution was granted and the tree was saved.

Given a little more time, Mr Boggie could have saved the tree by more orthodox methods. When a tree (or trees) is threatened with the chop, you can apply for a Tree Preservation Order under the Town and Country Planning Act. This makes it an offence, punishable by a £250 fine, to chop down any tree so protected.

How do you go about getting a Tree Preservation Order? The tree doesn't even have to be threatened. First, ring your local council and ask the Land Charges clerk if there is a TPO already in existence for that particular tree.

If not, ask to speak to the head of the Planning Department and say you wish to apply for a TPO; if there is

TIMBER!

an immediate danger of the tree being felled, a 'provisional' order will be made, taking effect immediately, pending a Ministry inquiry.

Fortunately, trees have many good friends who will be only too happy to rally to your support: after all, you can't put a tree back once it's been chopped down.

Write to the Civic Trust explaining your problem – they advise you and put you in touch with a nearby preservation society. There's also an organization called Men of the Trees, who are the Robin Hoods of the tree world. Fire off a letter to the Council for the Protection of Rural England, too.

All this takes time, of course – and if the axe is poised over the victim's trunk, the reprieve may come too late. In which case, like Mr Boggie, you will have to resort to guerrilla tactics. Stage a sit-in up a tree. Chain yourself to the trunk like some Swedish conservationists did in a Stockholm park a couple of years ago. Call the news editor and picture editor of a couple of national newspapers. They love a good weeping willow story.

When a number of trees are to be cut down, leaving some standing, it is the normal practice for the executioners to mark the condemned trees with an 'X' the day before sentence is carried out. By marking all the other trees with identical 'X's, you will confuse the enemy and cause long bureaucratic delays.

WARD'S LAW: You Tarzan, him no chop down tree.

VETS

Vets are bound by much the same professional code of conduct as doctors. That is to say, they are expected to treat their 'patients' to the best of their ability, they mustn't go off and play golf, leaving behind a surgery full of dying patients, and if they are discovered *in flagrante delicto* with a 'patient', they are of course struck off.

But here the similarities end. There is no Health Service for pets. The 'patients' can't complain if they are badly treated. And when an animal or a bird dies because of a vet's negligence, the animal relatives can't sue.

Most disputes between pet owners and vets are over money. Because medical treatment in Britain is free, there is a feeling that our dumb friends also ought to enjoy this privilege. And because most of us aren't used to paying our doctors, pet owners seem to think they shouldn't have to pay a vet if the treatment isn't successful. Alas, life isn't so kind.

It's the vet's experience, time and overheads you are paying for, and pretty expensive they are, too. But in return you are entitled to expect the very best and sympathetic treatment for your pet. Many pet-owners feel they are short-changed here.

The vet's equivalent to the General Medical Council is the Royal College of Veterinary Surgeons of which every vet practising in Britain is a member. The Royal College has a Disciplinary Committee, but complaining to it is about as rewarding as trying to teach your dog to talk. Out of 15,000 vets practising in this country, it hears only three or four cases a year.

There is a reason for this. Most pet lovers' complaints about vets allege negligence. *But the Royal College will not investigate cases of alleged negligence!* That, it says, is a matter for the courts.

In the case of the death of a valuable racehorse or a Cruft's winner, it would obviously be worth taking a chance and going to law to sue a vet. But most pets, though much beloved, are no Cruft's winners. It leaves the bereaved pet owner no recourse at all.

Worse than that even. YOU might end up being the one who is sued – by the vet. Some complainants have received a letter back from the Royal College saying that their complaint will be passed on to the vet concerned, but warning them that 'it is open to the veterinarian to put the matter in the hands of his solicitor if he considers the complaint defamatory'.

Don't let this put you off writing to the College, but

make sure that everything in your letter is scrupulously accurate and that you can prove it.

The College will, however, consider complaints involving 'professional misconduct', which can be widely interpreted as 'not playing the game'.

Mrs Marjorie Fitzsimmons, for instance, reported a vet who dumped the dead body of her cat on the doorstep of the family home in Plumstead, East London, because he was angry at being kept waiting for his £1 fee for putting the poor animal to sleep. The vet was found guilty of disgraceful professional conduct and severely reprimanded.

If you feel your vet might have been guilty of professional misconduct, write to the Registrar saying so. Give him all the relevant facts and ask that your complaints should be 'considered by the Preliminary Investigation Committee with a view to going before the Disciplinary Committee'. If you can get a solicitor or your MP to write the letter, all the better, because it will carry more weight.

The Disciplinary Committee has the power to strike off a vet it considers to be guilty of gross professional misconduct; or it might deliver a severe reprimand. Either way, you owe it to your budgie to seek some posthumous redress.

WARD'S LAW: Give your vet a dog's life if he doesn't look after your dumb friend.

VIOLENCE

From time to time you will be sorely tempted to seize the enemy by the throat, post a petrol bomb through his letter box, jump on his car bonnet or knee him in the groin.

Don't.

WARD'S LAW: He who casts the first stone could get six months.

WHY ARE WE WAITING?

(or: how to fix a legally binding delivery date)

My Aunt Millie ordered three lovely bamboo garden chairs, which were delivered to her home on the morning of her funeral. Thank heavens the undertakers moved a little faster than the furniture shop.

You don't have to die before shops and manufacturers come up with goods you ordered a year or more ago, but, unless you are young and hearty, you might well do.

Shopkeepers are always optimistic enough about delivery dates when you place the order and part with your money. It's only later that they tell you about the strike at the works, the fowl-pest sweeping Botswana and the world shortage of tennis balls, all of which are supposed to be depriving you of the quilted bedspread you were promised for last Christmas.

And, in the meantime, the shopkeeper enjoys an interest-free loan of your money.

What can you do to hold shopkeepers and manufacturers to their promises?

When you place an order, make it clear (preferably in writing) that you must have the goods by a certain date. When they don't arrive in time (as they almost certainly won't) you can then cancel the order, recover your deposit and claim damages for the inconvenience and expense to which you have been put.

You obviously can't do this if the shop refuses to give you a guaranteed delivery date. But you can't be expected to wait for ever, either. So when you feel your patience has been stretched to its limits, write to the shop giving them a deadline.

If they don't come up with the goods by then, you are entitled to cancel the order and recover your deposit.

This won't, of course, get you that micro-computerized stereophonic gas cooker you have coveted so grievously. But, as you cook your Sunday dinner over an open fire, you can console yourself with the thought that you will have struck a blow for downtrodden customers everywhere. And, of course, avenged the untimely demise of my Aunt Millie.

WARD'S LAW: They are fools who only stand and wait.

FRIENDS OF
COMPLAINERS

There are literally hundreds of organizations to which you can turn for help and advice in your fight against mindless and inefficient bureaucracy, or sharp practice in trading.

Some are trade associations. Others are organized by consumer protection groups. Others are organizations set up by the State for our protection.

GOVERNMENT FAIR-PLAY DEPARTMENTS

1. *The Ombudsman.* (Or, to give him his full titles, Parliamentary Commissioner for Administration, and Health Service Commissioner for England, Wales and Scotland.) He investigates complaints about administrative errors in Government departments, but you can only put your grievance to him through your MP. He has won some memorable victories against the Inland Revenue for oppressed tax-payers, but he's a bit of a Sir Galahad with a blunted sword because he does not have the power to investigate complaints involving local government, the Forces, police, magistrates, judges or anything that happens overseas. His name is Cecil Montacute Clothier, QC.

As Health Service Commissioner, wearing his other hat, he can investigate complaints about the National Health Service without the intervention of an MP. Write to him at Church House, Great Smith Street, London SW1.

2. *The Local Commissioner.* He – or, rather, they – are the Ombudsman's local-government equivalent. There are,

in fact, *four* local Commissioners who investigate complaints about maladministration – i.e. the *way* something has been done, as opposed to *what* was done. Their brief is too narrow, their powers fairly non-existent, but when all else has failed you have nothing to lose by getting in touch. Your complaint is supposed to be passed on to the Local Commissioner through a councillor, but if your councillor lets you down, you can contact the Commissioner direct. Write to: The Local Commissioner, 21 Queen Anne's Gate, London SW1 [England], or The Local Commissioner for Wales, Portland House, 22 Newport Road, Cardiff.

3. *The Director-General of Fair Trading*. He's the consumer's guard dog. His department has changed laws, leaned on corporations and street traders to drop sharp practices and investigated everything from Tupperware parties to washing-machine service contracts. His office produces many excellent and informative leaflets covering just about every possible disaster and pitfall you are likely to encounter. He can't fight individual battles, but keep him in touch with what's going on by writing to him at the Office of Fair Trading, Field House, Breams Buildings, London EC4 (01-242 2858).

4. *Minister of State for Consumer Affairs* (Mrs Sally Oppenheim). She's Mrs Thatcher's Queen of the High Street, responsible for a wide range of consumer problems. She'll probably bounce any problems you send her straight on to the Director General of Fair Trading, but the more she knows the better for us all. Write to her at the Department of Trade, 1 Victoria Street, London SW1.

5. *The National Consumer Council*. A Government-funded watchdog that has been known to bite the hand that feeds it. It does not pursue individual complaints, but – in the words of the Government White Paper – it 'makes representations of the consumer view to central and local government, to the Director of Fair Trading, to industry and

to any other quarter where the consumer voice ought to be heeded'. Education, transport, prices, housing . . . it makes everything its business. Write to the Director, Jeremy Mitchell, 18 Queen's Gate, London SW1 (01-222 9501).

CITIZENS' ADVICE BUREAUX

There are more than seven hundred of these veritable mines of information and help in Britain. Some are better than others, obviously, but I'd be very surprised if you had a problem they couldn't help you with. Look up the address of the nearest bureau in the telephone book, or write to the National Headquarters of the Citizens' Advice Bureaux, 26 Bedford Square, London WC1.

NEIGHBOURHOOD ADVICE CENTRES

More than two hundred of these help centres have sprung up during the last few years. They'll involve themselves totally in your problem, whatever it is. Good on welfare law. Not so good on broken toasters.

LEGAL ADVICE CENTRES

Many areas have free Legal Advice Centres (sometimes called Law Centres) where you can get advice about social and consumer problems. Sometimes they are run by the local council in conjunction with the Citizens' Advice Bureau. Sometimes they are manned voluntarily by lawyers interested in social work. The problem is finding out where they are and when they are open.

The Citizens' Advice Bureau should know if there is one in your area, but, if they don't, then you can try writing to the Legal Action Group, an independent organization set up to encourage the legal profession to provide more help in poor urban areas. Write to them at 28A Highgate Road, London NW5 (01-485 1189), but enclose a stamped, addressed envelope because, just as you need help, they need money.

CONSUMER ADVICE CENTRES

High Street centres where you can find out all the pros and cons about various consumer products, credit, insurance, or housing *before* you buy. If they are too late to prevent you making a mistake, they will also advise you on how best to fight your consumer battle of the week. The Consumer Advice Centre in Croydon recovered more than £30,000 for complainants in its first year. To find out if there is one in your area, ring the Trading Standards Officer at the Town Hall, or, again, ask your local Citizens' Advice Bureau.

CONSUMER ORGANIZATIONS

The Consumers' Association won't fight members' battles for them, but it's still a powerful crusader through its monthly magazine, *Which?*, which is crammed with good advice that will save you a lot of trouble and money. (There are other consumer-help magazines, such as *Motoring Which?* and *Money Which?*) By feeding the Association with your disastrous experiences from time to time you are helping the Association prevent others from falling flat on their faces, too. Write to them at 14 Buckingham Street, London WC2, for details of membership.

Many organizations that can offer help have been mentioned in this book, and the addresses and telephone numbers follow in the index at the back of the book. Here are some other trade and other organizations that you might be glad to know about some time.

CENTRAL HEATING
Heating & Ventilating Contractors' Association
Esca House, 34 Palace Court, London W2 (01-229 2488)

CIVIL RIGHTS
National Council for Civil Liberties
186 King's Cross Road, London WC1 (01-278 3259)

COAL

Domestic Coal Consumers' Council
Dean Bradley House, Horseferry Road, London SW1
(01-212 0093)

ELECTRICAL GOODS

Radio, Electrical and Television Retailers' Association
57–61 Newington Causeway, London SE1 (01-403 1463)
British Electrical and Allied Manufacturers' Association
Leicester House, 8 Leicester Street, London WC2
(01-437 0678)

ENVIRONMENT

Civic Trust
17 Carlton House Terrace, London SW1 (01-930 0914)
Ramblers' Association
1–4 Crawford Mews, York Street, London W1
(01-262 1477)

FOOD

The UK Association of Frozen Food Producers
1 Green Street, London W1 (01-629 0655)
The Food Manufacturers' Federation
6 Catherine Street, London WC2 (01-836 2460)

FURNITURE

The National Association of Retail Furnishers
3 Berners Street, London W1 (01-636 1778)

HAIRDRESSERS

The Hairdressing Council
17 Spring Street, London W2 (01-402 6367)

HEARING AIDS

Royal National Institute for the Deaf
105 Gower Street, London WC1 (01-387 8033)

HIRE PURCHASE
Consumer Credit Trade Association
3 Berners Street, London W1 (01-636 7564)

PAINTERS AND DECORATORS
The British Decorators Association
6 Haywra Street, Harrogate, Yorkshire (0423-67292)

PLUMBERS
National Association of Plumbing, Heating, and
    Mechanical Services Contractors
6 Gate Street, London WC2 (01-405 2678)

VENDING MACHINES
Automatic Vending Association of Great Britain
50 Eden Street, Kingston-on-Thames, Surrey
(01-549 7311)

INDEX OF ADDRESSES

British Gas Corporation
Chairman: 59 Bryanston Street, London W1 (01-723 7030)
Service Director: 326 High Holborn, London WC1
(01-242 0789)

British Insurance Brokers Association
Fountain House, 130 Fenchurch Street, London EC3
(01-623 9043)

British Insurance Association
Aldermary House, Queen Street, London EC4 (01-248 4477)

British Railways Board
222 Marylebone Road, London NW1 (01-262 3232)

British Standards Institute
2 Park Street, London W1 (01-629 9000)

British Transport Hotels Ltd
St Pancras Chambers, Euston Road, London NW1
(01-387 2878)

Caledonian Associated Cinemas Ltd
4 Academy Street, Inverness (0463-37611)

Civic Trust
17 Carlton House Terrace, London SW1 (01-930 0914)

Civil Aeronautics Board
1825 Connecticut Avenue, NY 20428, USA

Commission for Racial Equality
Elliot House, 10–12 Allington Street, London SW1
(01-828 7022)

Confederation for the Advancement of State Education
   (CASE)
1 Windermere Avenue, Wembley, Middlesex (01-904 1722)

Companies House
55 City Road, London EC1 (01-253 9393)

Consumers' Association
14 Buckingham Street, London WC2 (01-839 1222)

Council for the Protection of Rural England
4 Hobart Place, London SW1 (01-235 4771)

Courage Ltd
Anchor Terrace, 1–15 Southwark Bridge Road, London SE1
(01-407 7676)

Department of Health & Social Security
Alexander Fleming House, Elephant & Castle, London SE1
(01-407 5522)

Electrical & Radio Trading Magazine
Dorset House, Stamford Street, London SE1 (01-261 8000)

Electricity Consumers' Council
North-west House, 119 Marylebone Road, London NW1
(01-724 3431)

Electricity Council
30 Millbank, London SW1 (01-834 2333)

EMI Cinemas & Leisure Group
30 Golden Square, London W1 (01-437 9234)

Equal Opportunities Commission
Overseas House, Quay Street, Manchester (061-833 9244)

General Dental Council
37 Wimpole Street, London W1 (01-486 2171)

General Medical Council
44 Hallam Street, London W1 (01-580 7642)

Grand Metropolitan (Watney, Mann & Truman Ltd)
The Brewery, 91 Brick Lane, London E1 (01-247 4300)

Health Service Commissioners
ENGLAND—*Church House, Great Smith Street, London SW1*
SCOTLAND—*71 George Street, Edinburgh*
WALES—*Queen's Court, Plymouth Street, Cardiff CF1 4DA*

Independent Broadcasting Authority
70 Brompton Road, London SW3 (01-584 7011)

Inland Revenue
Somerset House, Strand, London WC2 (01-438 6622)

Insurance Brokers Registration Council
15 St Helen's Place, London EC3 (01-588 4387)

Law Society
113 Chancery Lane, London WC2 (01-242 1222)

The Lay Observer
Royal Courts of Justice, Strand, London WC2
(01-405 7641)

London Transport Executive
55 Broadway, London SW1 (01-222 5600)

London Transport Passengers Committee
Room 33, 26 Old Queen Street, London SW1 (01-222 8777)

Lord Chancellor's Department
Court Business Section, Neville House, Page Street,
London SW1 (01-211 8596)

Men of the Trees
Crawley Down, Crawley, Sussex (0342-712536)

Motor Agents Association
Conciliation Service, 73 Park Street, Bristol (0272-293232)

National Bus Company
25 New Street Square, London EC4 (01-583 9177)
South-East Region: *4–14 Mount Sion, Tunbridge Wells,*
Kent (0892 39517)
Northern Region: *55 Coniscliffe Road, Darlington, Co.*
Durham (0325 55201)
Midlands and West: *67 Ombersley Street, Droitwich,*
Worcs (09057-5626)
Wales and the Marches: *Alliance House, 18–19 High Street,*
Cardiff (0222-398565)

National Confederation of Parent-Teacher Associations
1 White Avenue, Northfleet, Gravesend, Kent (0474-60618)

National House-Building Council
Chiltern Avenue, Amersham, Bucks (02403-4477)

National Tenants Organisation
189a Old Brompton Road, London SW5 (01-373 4963)

Newspaper Publishers Association
6 Bouverie Street, London EC4 (01-583 8132)

Noise Abatement Society
6 Old Bond Street, London W1 (01-493 5877)

Office of Fair Trading
  Field House, 15–25 Breams Buildings, London EC4
  (01-242 2858)
Patients Association
  11 Dartmouth Street, London SW1 (01-222 4992)
Post Office Users National Council
  Waterloo Bridge House, Waterloo Road, London SE1
  (01-928 9458)
Press Council
  1 Salisbury Square, London EC4 (01-353 1248)
Radio, Electrical and Television Retailers Association
  57–61 Newington Causeway, London SE1 (01-403 1463)
Rank Leisure Services
  7 Great Russell Street, London WC1 (01-580 2010)
Retail Trading Standards Association
  Avon House, 360 Oxford Street, London W1 (01-629 9314)
Royal Automobile Club
  83 Pall Mall, London SW1 (01-930 2345)
Royal College of Veterinary Surgeons
  32 Belgrave Square, London SW1 (01-235 4971)
Royal Institute of Chemistry
  30 Russell Square, London WC1 (01-580 3482)
Scottish & Newcastle Breweries Ltd
  Abbey Brewery, Holyrood Road, Edinburgh (031-556 2591)
Senate of the Inns of Court and the Bar
  11 South Square, Gray's Inn, London WC1 (01-242 0082)
Shelter
  157 Waterloo Road, London SE1 (01-633 9377)
Society of Motor Manufacturers and Traders
  Forbes House, Halkin Street, London SW1 (01-235 7000)
Whitbread & Co Ltd
  The Brewery, Chiswell Street, London EC1 (01-606 4455)